30 minute
vegetarian

30 minute
vegetarian

Cook modern vegetarian recipes
in 30 minutes or less with
delicious and varied ingredients
such as lemon grass, sun-dried
tomatoes, pimentos, sweet
potatoes, couscous, polenta,
ricotta, and blueberries.

Joanna Farrow
Photography by William Reavell

LAUREL
GLEN

First published in North America in 2000 by
Laurel Glen Publishing
An imprint of the Advantage Publishers Group
5880 Oberlin Drive, San Diego, CA 92121-4794
www.advantagebooksonline.com

All notations of errors or omissions should be addressed to Laurel Glen
Publishing, editorial department, at the above address. All other
correspondence (author inquiries, permissions and rights) concerning the
content of this book should be addressed to Hamlyn, an imprint of
Octopus Publishing Group Ltd., 2–4 Heron Quays, London E14 4JP.

ISBN   1-57145-674-0 (hardcover)
          1-57145-680-5 (paperback)

Library of Congress Cataloging-in-Publication Data available upon
request.

Printed in China.

1 2 3 4 5   00 01 02 03 04

Notes

1 Standard level spoon measurements are used in all recipes.
2 Eggs should be medium unless otherwise stated. The USDA
advises that eggs should not be consumed raw. This book
contains dishes made with raw or lightly cooked eggs. It is
prudent for more vulnerable people, such as pregnant and
nursing mothers, invalids, the elderly, babies, and young children,
to avoid uncooked or lightly cooked dishes made with eggs. Once
prepared, these dishes should be kept refrigerated and used
promptly.
3 Milk should be whole unless otherwise stated.
4 Fresh herbs should be used unless otherwise stated. If
unavailable, use dried herbs as an alternative, but halve the
quantities stated.
5 Pepper should be freshly ground black pepper unless otherwise
stated.
6 Ovens should be preheated to the specified temperature—if using
a convection oven, follow the manufacturer's instructions for
adjusting the time and the temperature.
7 This book includes dishes made with nuts and nut derivatives. It
is advisable for customers with known allergic reactions to nuts
and nut derivatives and those who may be potentially vulnerable
to these allergies, such as pregnant and nursing mothers, invalids,
the elderly, babies, and children, to avoid dishes made with nuts
and nut oils. It is also prudent to check the labels of preprepared
ingredients for the possible inclusion of nut derivatives.
8 Vegetarians should look for special labeling on cheese to ensure
that it is made with vegetarian rennet. There are vegetarian forms
of Parmesan, feta, cheddar, Cheshire, Red Leicester, dolcelatte and
many goat cheeses, among others.

Executive Editor: Polly Manguel
Project Editor: Sarah Ford
Copy-editor: Jo Richardson
Creative Director: Keith Martin
Senior Designer: David Godfrey
Production Controller: Lisa Moore
Photographer: William Reavell
Stylist: Clare Hunt
Home Economist: Joanna Farrow

North American Edition
Publisher: Allen Orso
Managing Editor: JoAnn Padgett
Project Editor: Elizabeth McNulty

contents

6 introduction

8 glossary

10 soups
From light, elegant starters to comforting main-course soups.

22 pasta & noodles
Delicious Mediterranean pastas and exotic noodle dishes with all the flavors of the East.

34 beans & legumes
These versatile standbys are used in koftas, pâtés, purées, stews, and patties to make a satisfying feast.

46 rice
Rich, creamy risottos, sweet and spicy pilafs, and aromatic oriental rice dishes.

58 pizza & bread
Tempting recipes for crispy homemade pizzas, tortilla wraps, and crunchy bruschetta.

68 pancakes & pastries
Batter pancakes, vegetable rosti, succulent tartlets, and crisp phyllo pockets.

80 couscous, polenta, and grains
Inventive accompaniments and tasty main dishes using couscous, polenta, bulgur, and millet.

90 salads & side salads
A crisp, colorful array of main-course salads and side dishes.

100 vegetable dishes
With creative treatment, vegetables take center stage in a selection of mouth-watering recipes.

114 desserts & baked goods
Irresistible desserts and home baking for a little sweet indulgence.

126 index

introduction

30 Minute Vegetarian will appeal to anyone who knows how exotic and exciting contemporary vegetarian cooking can be.

Like many children of my generation, I was raised on a meat-based diet, but even then I found a traditional roast dinner or a classic winter stew rather difficult to swallow, despite my mother's evident cooking skills. I have memories of trying to hide unwanted pieces of beef or lamb under my knife and fork in the naive hope that my parents would not notice. This was possibly a taste of things to come for me personally, but maybe the reality is that most of us have moved away from a "meat and two veggies" diet.

This is, of course, an inevitable consequence of the explosion of interest in all things relating to food. We travel more and seize the opportunity to sample different cuisines, new flavors, and ingredients that were completely alien to our parents. There is also now a far greater variety of foods widely available, gathered from the all over the world. Television programs, food magazines and cookbooks all fuel our desire to enjoy an ever-widening feast of interesting flavors.

All this has helped the vegetarian cause tremendously. Moral issues aside, people have discovered that there are so many nonmeat-based cuisines around the globe from which to draw new inspiration, and so meat (like my mother's roasts) has been pushed aside. How many people eat as much meat as they did even ten years ago?

My aim in this book is to show that vegetarian cooking has thrown off its dull yet worthy image for good, epitomized by the token vegetable lasagna or the equally dreary vegetarian alternatives that some restaurants used to (and still do in some cases) offer. Whether you are a confirmed vegetarian or a carnivore seeking a fresh approach, here is a collection of recipes to excite and delight—a heady mix of stimulating flavors and diverse culinary practices. And it is all fast food! It takes so little time to whip up a delicious homemade pesto and toss it with pasta, or to throw a blend of aromatic Far Eastern spices in a pan with beans and vegetables, then pile them on top of noodles. This spontaneity captures the essence of fresh herbs and the pungency of spices to create imaginative, flavorful dishes in less than 30 minutes. Yes, you might have to plan what you are going to cook a little more, and yes, it might mean using a few more ingredients, but it certainly will not involve your spending hours in the kitchen assembling complicated or expensive creations.

For anyone who is yet to be convinced about the value of vegetarian cooking, think of your meat-based diet as a habit. Once you break the habit of meat-eating, it is not necessarily a case of giving up anything but opening yourself up to a wealth of new, vibrant, and easy ways of cooking.

Joanna Farrow

glossary

Balsamic vinegar
This has been a popular ingredient for some years now, with a far richer, sweeter flavor than ordinary wine vinegars. It is made in Modena, Italy and is aged in wooden barrels for anything up to 50 years, the maturing time developing its flavor—and price!

Cheese
Cheese plays an important role in vegetarian cooking, not purely as a flavoring but as a useful source of protein, calcium, and vitamins. While many vegetarians will eat nonvegetarian cheeses, others avoid them because of the presence of rennet used to solidify many cheeses. In recent years, there has been a huge increase in the amount of cheeses produced using vegetarian rennet. The difference in taste is barely discernible and it behaves no differently when used in cooking.

Brie and camembert: These are encased in a soft, white penicillin mold and vary considerably from dry and crumbly to runny and strongly flavored. Sliced, they can be lightly grilled and tossed with pasta or used as a topping for toast, pizzas, or pastries.

Dolcelatte: This soft, creamy, blue-veined Italian cheese made from cow's milk is a milder version of Gorgonzola.

Haloumi: This firm, salty Greek cheese has a dense, chewy texture that is delicious broiled or fried and tossed into salads. It goes particularly well with fruit such as grapes and pears.

Mascarpone: A deliciously soft, velvet-smooth cream cheese made with cows' milk. It is good in savory dishes since it melts to create wonderfully rich sauces, as well as in sweet dishes as a creamy trifle or tiramisu base.

Mozzarella: A fresh, moist, subtle-flavored cheese, made from either buffalo or cows' milk. It has an inviting stringy quality when melted and is often combined with more intensely flavored cheeses such as Parmesan to add flavor. Excellent on pizzas or pastries, or in salads.

Parmesan: A strongly flavored hard, salty cheese which is matured for years to develop the full flavor. Always buy in a block rather than already-grated. Leftovers can be grated and frozen.

Ricotta: A soft, bland, fresh cheese that is often stirred into pasta or used in pastry fillings. It is also good as a quick and easy dessert, mixed with chocolate, ginger, dried fruit, and liqueurs.

Chilies
These vary considerably in heat intensity and unfortunately there is often no way of knowing how hot they are until you cook them. The tiny Thai chilies, both red and green, are always very fiery, while the larger, chubbier chilies, usually sold loose in supermarkets, tend to be milder. Sometimes more unusual chilies, such as Scotch Bonnet and Habañero, are available in small packs, usually labeled as to heat intensity.

Coconut
Once you have mastered the art of opening a fresh coconut, the grated flesh adds a refreshing, nutty flavor to salads and stir-fries. To open the coconut, first pierce the three "eyes" with a skewer (sometimes a corkscrew works well) and drain the juice into a mug. Some people love this nutritious, opaque juice, while others hate it! Place the coconut in a plastic bag and beat with a hammer to crack it into several pieces. Ease out the flesh from the shell.

Coconut milk
This is not the juice from inside the whole coconut, but a thick, velvety smooth, creamy milk that is processed from coconut flesh. Sold in cans and cartons, it is one of the most widely used cooking liquids in Southeast Asian and Caribbean cookery, and excellent for giving "body" and richness to vegetarian soups, stews and oriental dishes.

Creamed coconut
Very concentrated in flavor, a small chunk (about 1–2 oz) can be added to soups, stews, and sauces to thicken and intensify flavor. Creamed coconut melts as it heats up.

Lemon grass
This is now widely available fresh and adds a wonderful, aromatic, lemony flavor to soups and spicy dishes. Peel away any tough, discolored leaves, then finely slice or chop the rest. If you cannot find fresh lemon grass, look for it dried in jars with the other spices.

Noodles
There are many different types of noodles available, from rice noodles to those made from wheat, bean starch, and buckwheat. Some are thick and ribbon-like, while others are fine like vermicelli. They generally cook very quickly, and rice noodles will turn mushy and paste-like if overcooked.

Olive oil
Extra virgin olive oil comes from the first cold pressing of the olives, giving a rich flavor and deep color. Subsequent pressings produce oils of a lighter flavor. It is worth keeping an extra-virgin olive oil for salad dressings and dishes in which you want an intense, Mediterranean flavor, and a lighter, cheaper one for other cooking and for frying.

You can easily make your own flavored oils by steeping sprigs of rosemary, tarragon, thyme, bay leaves, or some whole fresh chilies in the oil for a few weeks before using.

Pasta
This is a blend of flour and water,

sometimes with the addition of egg. Fresh pasta has a better flavor and texture than dried and cooks very quickly, usually in less time than package directions suggest, so take care when cooking. Leftover fresh pasta can be frozen successfully.

Dried pasta makes a good pantry alternative but brands vary considerably in quality. When draining any cooked pasta, always leave the last of the cooking water clinging to the pasta, to prevent the dish being dry.

Pesto

This is a blend of basil, pine nuts, Parmesan cheese, garlic, and oil which can be bought in jars or, preferably, homemade. Simply put a clove of chopped garlic, a handful of basil leaves, 3 tbsp. pine nuts, and 2 oz. grated Parmesan cheese in a food processor or blender and process, gradually adding a little olive oil, to make a thick, oily paste. Pesto is delicious simply tossed with pasta for a quick and easy supper, or stirred into soups and sauces. Red pesto has the addition of tomatoes.

Sun-dried tomato pesto (see page 65) makes a delicious variation on the pesto theme.

Polenta

This is made from ground corn kernels and is cooked by blending with water to make a thick paste. Serve it soft, rather like mashed potatoes, or spread on a tray, let set, then slice for broiling or baking, preferably with a cheese topping. Its bland flavor can be enhanced by the addition of garlic, olive oil, herbs, saffron, or chilies. Buy packs labeled "instant polenta," which cooks much faster.

Rice

There are dozens of varieties available. Most cook quickly, making a useful alternative to pasta and potatoes, although some varieties of red, brown, and "wild" rice take much longer. For spicy dishes, choose white or brown basmati or Thai fragrant rice, which has a softer, fluffier texture and better flavor than ordinary long-grain rice. Italian risotto rices, either arborio or carnaroli, are very popular for making classic, creamy risottos. Flavor with mushrooms, asparagus, or simply cheese for a quick and easy vegetarian meal.

Arugula

This is a delicious peppery-tasting salad leaf. Try growing your own rather than buying ridiculously expensive packs. Plant some in a pot or in the garden monthly through the summer for a cheap and far more flavorful supply.

Saffron

It is very expensive, but saffron adds a distinctive flavor and color to many dishes that no other spice can imitate. It is perfect for Mediterranean rice and bean dishes, or for adding to polenta and potatoes.

Sun-dried tomatoes

These intensely flavored dried tomatoes, usually bought in oil, are so useful in northern climates where ordinary tomatoes lack the color and sweet flavor of those grown around the Mediterranean. Chopped up, they are great for adding flavor intensity to tomato soups and stews. Sun-dried tomato paste is equally useful.

Tapenade

A paste-like blend of olives, garlic, capers, and olive oil that can be store-bought or made at home by simply blending 3 tbsp. capers, ½ cup pitted black olives, 6 tbsp. olive oil and a little garlic, herbs, and seasoning. If buying, check that the brand does not contain anchovies.

Tofu

Made from soy beans and sold in block form, tofu is bland in both taste and appearance, but should not be disregarded. Its assets are its nutritional value as a meat replacement and its great versatility in vegetarian cooking. Use it as a carrier for strongly flavored ingredients such as soy sauce, garlic, ginger, lemon grass, and spices. It is also available smoked.

Silken tofu is a lighter version of regular tofu. Easy to mash or blend, it is generally used in drinks and as a dairy replacement in desserts.

Vegetable stock

A vital ingredient in vegetarian soups, stews, casseroles, rice, and vegetable dishes. Liquid stock concentrate, bought in small jars, has a better flavor than the reconstituted cubes for everyday vegetarian cooking. For special occasions, buy fresh vegetable stock or make your own if you have time. Use the vegetables listed below as a guide, but throw in any other leftover trimmings such as cabbage, broccoli, zucchini, fennel, spring onions, or celeriac. Both the color and flavor of homemade vegetable stock is rich and intense.
Makes 3½ cups

2 tbsp. olive oil
1 large onion, chopped, plus skins
2 carrots, chopped
4 oz. turnip or parsnip
3 celery stalks, sliced
4 oz. mushrooms, sliced
2 bay leaves
several thyme and parsley sprigs
2 tomatoes, chopped
2 tsp. black peppercorns

one Heat the oil in a large saucepan. Add the onion, carrots, turnip or parsnip, celery, and mushrooms and sauté gently for 5 minutes. Add the herbs, tomatoes, peppercorns, and onion skins and cover with 6 cups water. **two** Bring to a boil, partially cover, and simmer gently for 1 hour. Cool, then strain and refrigerate for up to 2 days.

soups

Soups are without doubt among the easiest, most comforting ways to enjoy vegetarian food. Generous portions thick with chunky vegetables or legumes and served with warm, grainy bread make really satisfying main meal dishes, while smoothly blended, light, and fragrant versions whet the appetite for a delicious meal to follow.

Preparation time 5 minutes Cooking time 20 minutes Total time 25 minutes Serves 4

lima bean and sun-dried tomato soup

3 tbsp. olive oil
1 onion, finely chopped
2 celery stalks, thinly sliced
2 garlic cloves, thinly sliced
two 14 oz. cans lima beans, rinsed and drained
4 tbsp. sun-dried tomato paste
3 cups Vegetable Stock (see page 9)
1 tbsp. chopped rosemary or thyme
salt and pepper
Parmesan shavings, to serve

Although it takes only a few minutes to prepare, this chunky soup distinctly resembles a robust Italian minestrone. It makes a worthy main course served with bread and plenty of Parmesan.

one Heat the oil in a saucepan. Add the onion and sauté for 3 minutes until softened. Add the celery and garlic and sauté for 2 minutes.

two Add the lima beans, sun-dried tomato paste, stock, rosemary or thyme, and a little salt and pepper. Bring to a boil, then reduce the heat, cover, and simmer gently for 15 minutes. Serve sprinkled with Parmesan shavings.

Preparation time 7 minutes Cooking time 23 minutes Total time 30 minutes Serves 4

green lentil soup with spiced butter

3 tbsp. olive oil
2 onions, sliced
2 bay leaves
6 oz. green lentils, rinsed
3½ cups Vegetable Stock (see page 9)
½ tsp. ground turmeric
small handful of cilantro leaves, coarsely chopped
salt and pepper

Spiced butter
2 tbsp. lightly salted butter, softened
1 large garlic clove, crushed
1 tsp. paprika
1 tsp. cumin seeds
1 red chili, seeded and thinly sliced

Serve the spicy butter separately for stirring into the soup, so that can each person can "heat up" their own portion according to personal taste.

one Heat the oil in a saucepan. Add the onions and sauté for 3 minutes. Add the bay leaves, lentils, stock, and turmeric. Bring to a boil, then reduce the heat, cover, and simmer for 20 minutes or until the lentils are tender and turning mushy.

two Meanwhile, to prepare the spiced butter, beat the butter with the garlic, paprika, cumin seeds, and chili and transfer to a small serving dish.

three Stir the cilantro into the soup, season to taste with salt and pepper, and serve with the spiced butter in a separate bowl at the table for stirring into the soup.

black bean soup with soba noodles

7 oz. dried soba noodles
2 tbsp. peanut or vegetable oil
1 bunch of scallions, sliced
2 garlic cloves, coarsely chopped
1 red chili, seeded and sliced
1½ inch piece of fresh ginger, peeled and grated
½ cup black bean sauce or black bean stir-fry sauce
1½ cups Vegetable Stock (see page 9)
7 oz. bok choy or spring greens, shredded
2 tsp. soy sauce
1 tsp. sugar
½ cup raw, unsalted shelled peanuts

Soba noodles, traditional in Japanese cooking, are made of buckwheat and whole-wheat flour, giving them a nutty flavor without the dryness of many whole-wheat pastas.

one Cook the noodles in plenty of boiling water for about 5 minutes or until just tender.

two Meanwhile, heat the oil in a saucepan. Add the scallions and garlic and sauté gently for 1 minute.

three Add the chili, ginger, black bean sauce, and stock and bring to a boil. Stir in the bok choy or spring greens, soy sauce, sugar, and peanuts, reduce the heat and simmer gently, uncovered, for 4 minutes.

four Drain the noodles and pile into serving bowls. Ladle the soup over the noodles and serve immediately.

new potato, cilantro, and leek soup

1 lb. waxy new potatoes, such as Jersey Royals, scrubbed
3 small leeks, trimmed
1½ tbsp. butter
1 tbsp. black mustard seeds
1 onion, chopped
1 garlic clove, thinly sliced
3½ cups Vegetable Stock (see page 9)
plenty of freshly grated nutmeg
small handful of cilantro, coarsely chopped
salt and pepper
warm bread, to serve

one Halve each potato, or cut into ½ inch slices if large. Halve the leeks lengthwise, then cut across into thin shreds.

two Melt the butter in a heavy-bottomed saucepan. Add the mustard seeds, onion, garlic, and potatoes and sauté gently for 5 minutes. Add the stock and nutmeg and bring just to a boil. Reduce heat, cover, and simmer gently for about 10 minutes or until the potatoes are just tender.

three Stir in the leeks and cilantro and cook for a 5 minutes more. Season to taste with salt and pepper and serve with warm bread.

Preparation time 5 minutes Cooking time 20 minutes Total time 25 minutes Serves 4

spinach and mushroom soup

2 tbsp. butter
1 tbsp. peanut or vegetable oil
1 onion, finely chopped
5 oz. shiitake mushrooms
6 oz. chestnut or cup mushrooms
2 garlic cloves, crushed
2 inch piece of fresh ginger, peeled and grated
3½ cups Vegetable Stock (see page 9)
7½ oz. baby spinach
plenty of freshly grated nutmeg
salt and pepper
croûtons, to serve

one Melt the butter with the oil in a large saucepan. Add the onion and sauté for 5 minutes. Add the mushrooms and garlic and sauté for 3 minutes.

two Stir in the ginger and stock. Bring to a boil, then reduce the heat, cover, and simmer gently for 10 minutes.

three Add the spinach and nutmeg and simmer gently for 2 minutes. Season to taste with salt and pepper and serve scattered with croûtons.

Preparation time 5 minutes Cooking time 15 minutes Total time 20 minutes Serves 4

creamed corn and potato soup

2 tbsp. olive oil
1 onion, chopped
2 celery stalks, thinly sliced
3½ cups Vegetable Stock (see page 9)
13 oz. potatoes, diced
10 oz. frozen corn
2 tbsp. chopped tarragon
plenty of freshly grated nutmeg
4 tbsp. heavy cream
salt and pepper

one Heat the oil in a large saucepan. Add the onion and celery and sauté gently for 5 minutes. Add the stock and bring to a boil.

two Add the potatoes, reduce the heat and simmer, uncovered, for 5 minutes. Add the corn and tarragon, cover and simmer for 5 minutes more or until the potatoes are tender.

three Transfer the soup to a food processor or blender and process until pulpy but not smooth, or leave the soup in the pan and use a hand-held electric blender.

four Return the soup to the pan, if necessary, and add the nutmeg and cream. Season to taste with salt and pepper and heat through gently for 1 minute before serving.

fresh ginger and parsnip soup

1 tbsp. butter
one 4 in. piece fresh ginger, peeled and thinly sliced
1 bunch of scallions
1 lb. parsnips, sliced
3½ cups Vegetable Stock (see page 9)
salt and pepper
crème fraîche, to serve

one Melt the butter in a saucepan, add the ginger, and sauté gently for 1 minute. Reserve 1 scallion. Coarsely chop the remainder and add to the pan with the parsnips. Sauté gently for 2 minutes.

two Add the stock and bring to a boil. Reduce the heat, cover, and simmer gently for 15 minutes or until the parsnips are tender. Meanwhile, shred the reserved scallion lengthwise into fine ribbons.

three Transfer the soup to a food processor or blender and process until smooth, or leave the soup in the pan and use a hand-held electric blender.

four Return the soup to the pan, if necessary, season to taste with salt and pepper and heat through gently for 1 minute, then ladle into soup bowls. Serve topped with a spoonful of crème fraîche scattered with scallion ribbons.

Preparation time 5 minutes Cooking time 15 minutes Total time 20 minutes Serves 4

garlic and paprika soup with a floating egg

4 tbsp. olive oil
12 thick slices of French bread
5 garlic cloves, sliced
1 onion, finely chopped
1 tbsp. paprika
1 tsp. ground cumin
good pinch of saffron threads
4 cups Vegetable Stock (see page 9)
1 oz. dried soup pasta
4 eggs
salt and pepper

This is based on a Spanish soup in which the eggs are poached or oven-baked in a rich, garlicky broth. Here, pasta is added to give a little more substance to the dish.

one Heat the oil in a heavy-bottomed saucepan. Add the bread and sauté gently, turning once, until golden. Drain on paper towels.

two Add the garlic, onion, paprika, and cumin and sauté gently for 3 minutes. Add the saffron and stock and bring to a boil. Stir in the soup pasta. Reduce the heat, cover, and simmer for about 8 minutes or until the pasta is just tender. Season to taste with salt and pepper.

three Break the eggs on to a saucer and slide into the pan one at a time. Cook for about 2 minutes until poached.

four Stack 3 fried bread slices in each of 4 soup bowls. Ladle the soup over the bread, making sure each serving contains an egg. Serve immediately.

Preparation time 10 minutes Cooking time 20 minutes Total time 30 minutes Serves 4

creamed shallot and rosemary soup

4 tbsp. olive oil
12 oz. shallots, sliced
1 red onion, coarsely chopped
2 garlic cloves, coarsely chopped
4 large rosemary sprigs
1 tsp. sugar
2½ cups Vegetable Stock (see page 9)
5 tbsp. heavy cream
salt and pepper
toasted French bread croûtons, to serve

one Heat the oil in a saucepan. Add the shallots, onion, garlic, rosemary, and sugar and sauté gently for about 5 minutes or until softened and lightly browned.

two Add the stock and bring to a boil. Reduce the heat, cover, and simmer gently for about 15 minutes or until the shallots are tender.

three Transfer the soup to a food processor or blender and process until smooth, or leave the soup in the pan and use a hand-held electric blender.

four Return the soup to the pan, if necessary, stir in the cream, and season to taste with salt and pepper. Heat through gently for 1 minute, ladle into soup bowls, and serve sprinkled with croûtons.

Preparation time 5 minutes   Cooking time 12 minutes   Total time 17 minutes   Serves 4

pumpkin and coconut soup

3 tbsp. peanut oil
4 thyme sprigs
2 garlic cloves, coarsely chopped
1 red chili, seeded and coarsely chopped
1 tsp. cumin seeds
14 oz. can solid-pack pumpkin
1 tbsp. dark brown sugar
1½ cups Vegetable Stock (see page 9)
14 oz. can coconut milk
1–2 tbsp. lemon or lime juice
salt and pepper
coarsely chopped cilantro, to garnish

one Heat the oil in a saucepan. Strip the thyme leaves from the sprigs and add to the oil with the garlic, chili, and cumin seeds. Sauté gently for 2 minutes.

two Add the pumpkin, sugar, stock, and coconut milk and bring to a boil. Reduce the heat, cover, and simmer gently for 10 minutes.

three Add the lemon or lime juice, season to taste with salt and pepper, then serve scattered with the chopped cilantro.

Preparation time 10 minutes   Cooking time 15 minutes   Total time 25 minutes   Serves 4–6

chili and pimento soup

2 tbsp. olive oil
2 onions, chopped
2 garlic cloves, chopped
1 red chili, seeded and sliced
7 oz. jar pimentos, drained
1 lb. tomatoes, peeled
2 tsp. sugar
3½ cups Vegetable Stock (see page 9)
2 tbsp. chopped cilantro
4 tbsp. crème fraîche
salt and pepper

one Heat the oil in a large saucepan. Add the onions, garlic, and chili and sauté gently for 3 minutes.

two Add the pimentos, tomatoes, sugar, and stock and bring to a boil. Reduce the heat, cover, and simmer gently for about 10 minutes or until the tomatoes are soft.

three Transfer the soup to a food processor or blender and process until smooth, or leave the soup in the pan and use a hand-held electric blender.

four Return the soup to the pan, if necessary, and stir in the cilantro and crème fraîche. Season to taste with salt and pepper and heat through gently for 1 minute before serving.

zucchini and parmesan soup

1 tbsp. butter
1 tbsp. olive oil
1 large onion, chopped
15 oz. zucchini, sliced
¾ cup pine nuts
1 tbsp. chopped sage
3½ cups Vegetable Stock (see page 9)
3½ oz. Parmesan cheese, crumbled
4 tbsp. heavy cream
salt and pepper

one Melt the butter with the oil in a large saucepan. Add the onion, zucchini, and pine nuts and sauté gently for about 5 minutes or until softened.

two Add the sage and stock and bring to a boil. Reduce the heat, cover, and simmer gently for 5 minutes. Add the Parmesan cheese and cook for 2 minutes.

three Transfer the soup to a food processor or blender and process lightly until partially blended but not smooth, or leave the soup in the pan and use a hand-held electric blender.

four Return the soup to the pan, if necessary, and stir in the cream and a little salt and pepper. Heat through gently for 1 minute before serving.

pasta & noodles

The vast range of pasta and noodles available in supermarkets and specialty food stores is a bonus for all food lovers, particularly vegetarians. Opt for the more familiar Mediterranean approach with colorful vegetables and melting cheese or the exotic flavors of the East with egg noodle or rice noodle dishes.

Preparation time 5 minutes Cooking time 17 minutes Total time 22 minutes Serves 4–6

fettuccine with eggplant and pine nuts

8 tbsp. olive oil
2 medium eggplant, diced
2 red onions, sliced
3/4 cup pine nuts
3 garlic cloves, crushed
5 tbsp. sun-dried tomato paste
1/2 cup Vegetable Stock (see page 9)
10 oz. cracked pepper, tomato, or mushroom-
flavored fresh fettuccine
1 cup pitted black olives
salt and pepper
3 tbsp. coarsely chopped flat leaf parsley, to garnish

one Heat the oil in a large frying pan and sauté the eggplant and onions for 8–10 minutes until golden and tender. Add the pine nuts and garlic and sauté for 2 minutes. Stir in the sun-dried tomato paste and stock and cook for 2 minutes.

two Meanwhile, cook the pasta in plenty of lightly salted boiling water for about 2 minutes or until just tender.

three Drain the pasta and return to the pan. Add the sauce and olives, season to taste with salt and pepper and toss together over moderate heat for 1 minute until combined. Serve scattered with parsley.

Preparation time 5 minutes Cooking time 10 minutes Total time 15 minutes Serves 4

cherry tomato and ricotta penne

10 oz. dried penne
3 tbsp. olive oil
1 onion, chopped
4 garlic cloves, crushed
1 tbsp. chopped oregano
11 oz. cherry tomatoes, halved
1 tsp. sugar
3 tbsp. sun-dried tomato paste
1 cup ricotta cheese
salt and pepper

one Cook the pasta in plenty of lightly salted boiling water for about 10 minutes or until just tender.

two Meanwhile, heat the oil in a frying pan. Add the onion and sauté gently for 3 minutes. Add the garlic, oregano, tomatoes, and sugar and sauté quickly for 1 minute, stirring. Add the sun-dried tomato paste and 6 tbsp. of water, season to taste with salt and pepper, and bring to a boil. Place teaspoonfuls of the ricotta cheese into the pan and heat through gently for 1 minute.

three Drain the pasta and pile on to serving plates. Spoon the tomato and cheese mixture on top, taking care not to break up the ricotta too much. Serve immediately.

Preparation time 5 minutes Cooking time 5 minutes Total time 10 minutes Serves 4

pasta with watercress, dolcelatte, and walnut sauce

1 lb. fresh pasta shapes
³/₄ cup walnut pieces, toasted
6 oz. mature dolcelatte, diced
finely grated rind of 1 lemon
7 oz. crème fraîche
4 oz. watercress sprigs,
coarse stalks removed
salt and pepper

Like so many delicious pasta dishes, just a few simple ingredients are combined here to make an almost instant supper dish, fit for any occasion. If you are substituting dried pasta, use 10 oz. and cook it while you prepare the other ingredients. Serve with a tangy tomato and red onion salad.

one Cook the pasta in plenty of lightly salted boiling water for 2–3 minutes or until just tender. Drain lightly and return to the pan with the residual water still clinging to the pasta.

two Add the walnut pieces, cheese, lemon rind, crème fraîche, and watercress, and season to taste with salt and pepper.

three Toss the ingredients together over a low heat for 2 minutes until the crème fraîche has melted to make a sauce and the watercress has wilted. Serve immediately.

Preparation time 10 minutes Cooking time 5 minutes Total time 15 minutes Serves 4

fettuccine with tomatoes and tapenade

1 cup pitted black olives
1 red chili, seeded and sliced
4 tbsp. capers
2 tbsp. sun-dried tomato paste
3 tbsp. chopped basil
3 tbsp. chopped parsley or chervil
4 tomatoes, chopped
½ cup olive oil
12 oz. fresh fettuccine or fresh pasta shapes
salt and pepper
grated Parmesan cheese, to serve

one Place the olives, chili, and capers in a food processor or blender and process until quite finely chopped. Alternatively, finely chop them by hand. Mix with the sun-dried tomato paste, herbs, tomatoes, and oil, and season to taste with salt and pepper.

two Cook the pasta in plenty of lightly salted boiling water for 2–3 minutes until only just tender. Drain and return to the saucepan.

three Add the olive mixture and toss the ingredients together lightly over low heat for 2 minutes. Transfer to serving plates and serve sprinkled with Parmesan.

mushroom, zucchini, and mascarpone lasagna

1 oz. dried porcini mushrooms
3 tbsp. olive oil
4 oz. fresh lasagna sheets, halved
8 oz. mascarpone
2 garlic cloves, crushed
3 tbsp. chopped dill or tarragon
1 tbsp. butter
½ cup breadcrumbs
1 lb. button mushrooms, sliced
2 zucchini, sliced
salt and pepper

one Place the dried mushrooms in a bowl, cover with boiling water, and let stand while preparing the remaining ingredients.

two Bring a large saucepan of water to a boil with 1 tbsp. of the oil. Add the pasta sheets, one at a time, and cook for about 4 minutes or until just tender. Drain.

three Meanwhile, mix together in a small bowl the mascarpone, garlic, dill or tarragon, and season to taste with salt and pepper. Melt half the butter in a frying pan, add the breadcrumbs, and sauté gently for 2 minutes. Drain on paper towels.

four Melt the remaining butter in the pan with the remaining oil. Add the fresh mushrooms and zucchini and sauté for about 6 minutes or until golden. Drain the dried mushrooms, add to the pan, and sauté for 1 minute.

five Lay 4 pieces of lasagna, spaced slightly apart, in a shallow oven-proof dish. Spoon over a third of the vegetables, then a spoonful of the mascarpone mixture. Add another piece of lasagna to each stack and spoon over more vegetables and mascarpone. Finally, add the remaining lasagna, vegetables, and mascarpone.

six Scatter with the fried breadcrumbs and bake in a preheated, 400°F **oven for 6–8 minutes or until heated through.**

Preparation time 5 minutes Cooking time 7 minutes Total time 12 minutes Serves 4

goat cheese linguini with garlic and herb butter

10 oz. firm goat cheese
1 lemon
3 tbsp. butter
2 tbsp. olive oil
3 shallots, finely chopped
2 garlic cloves, crushed
1 oz. mixed chopped herbs, such as tarragon, chervil, parsley, dill
3 tbsp. capers
10 oz. fresh linguini or 8 oz. dried linguini
salt and pepper

If you cannot get fresh pasta for this dish, use dried and cook it while you make the sauce. Always drain the pasta lightly so that it retains plenty of moisture and does not dry out the sauce.

one Thickly slice the goat cheese and arrange on a lightly oiled, foil-lined broiler pan. Broil under a preheated broiler for about 2 minutes until golden. Keep warm.

two Peel strips of rind from the lemon, then squeeze the juice.

three Melt the butter in a frying pan with the oil. Add the shallots and garlic and sauté gently for 3 minutes. Stir in the herbs, capers, and lemon juice, and season to taste with salt and pepper.

four Cook the pasta in plenty of lightly salted boiling water for about 2 minutes or until just tender. Drain lightly and return to the saucepan. Add the goat cheese and herb butter and toss all the ingredients together gently. Serve scattered with the strips of lemon rind.

Preparation time 10 minutes Cooking time 12 minutes Total time 22 minutes Serves 4

stir-fried vegetable noodles

8 oz. medium egg noodles
4 tbsp. peanut oil
1 bunch of scallions, sliced
2 carrots, thinly sliced
2 garlic cloves, crushed
¼ tsp. dried chili flakes
4 oz. snow peas
4 oz. shiitake mushrooms, halved
3 Chinese cabbage leaves, shredded
2 tbsp. light soy sauce
3 tbsp. hoisin sauce

Just like pasta, noodles make a great pantry standby when you are at a loss for something to cook. More or less any salad vegetables from the refrigerator can be thrown in and simply zipped up with a splash of hoisin and soy sauce.

one Cook the noodles in lightly salted boiling water for about 4 minutes or until just tender. Drain.

two Heat the oil in a large frying pan or wok. Add the scallions and carrots and stir-fry for 3 minutes. Add the garlic, chili flakes, snow peas, and mushrooms and stir-fry for 2 minutes. Add the Chinese cabbage and stir-fry for 1 minute.

three Add the drained noodles to the pan with the soy sauce and hoisin sauce. Stir-fry over a gentle heat for 2 minutes until heated through. Serve immediately.

30. pasta & noodles

Preparation time 10 minutes Cooking time 10 minutes Total time 20 minutes Serves 4

vegetable noodles in spiced coconut milk

4 oz. dried medium egg noodles
2 tbsp. peanut or vegetable oil
1 onion, chopped
1 red chili, seeded and sliced
3 garlic cloves, sliced
2 inch piece of fresh ginger, peeled and grated
2 tsp. ground coriander
½ tsp. ground turmeric
1 stalk lemon grass, finely sliced
14 oz. can coconut milk
1 cup Vegetable Stock (see page 9)
4 oz. spring greens or cabbage, finely shredded
9 oz. runner beans or French beans, sliced diagonally
5 oz. shiitake mushrooms, sliced
3 oz. unsalted, shelled peanuts
salt and pepper

A single Thai chili gives this dish a really fiery kick. Substitute a mild chili if you are feeling cautious!

one Place the noodles in a bowl, cover with boiling water, and let stand while preparing the vegetables.

two Heat the oil in a large saucepan. Add the onion, chili, garlic, ginger, coriander, turmeric, and lemon grass and sauté gently for 5 minutes.

three Drain the noodles. Add the coconut milk and stock to the pan and bring just to a boil. Reduce the heat and stir in the spring greens or cabbage, beans, mushrooms, and drained noodles. Cover and simmer for 5 minutes. Stir in the peanuts and season to taste with salt and pepper, serve in deep bowls.

Preparation time 10 minutes Cooking time 5 minutes Total time 15 minutes Serves 4

rice noodles with green beans and ginger

3½ oz. fine rice noodles
4 oz. green beans, halved
finely grated rind and juice of 2 limes
1 Thai chili, seeded and finely chopped
1 inch piece of fresh ginger, peeled and finely chopped
2 tsp. sugar
small handful of chopped cilantro
½ cup dried pineapple pieces, chopped

This refreshing, slightly tangy starter makes a perfect prelude to any spicy, Far Eastern-style main course. Serve warm, or refresh the noodles and beans under cold running water to make a chilled alternative. To turn it into a main course for two, stir in some diced smoked tofu.

one Place the noodles in a bowl, cover with plenty of boiling water, and leave for 4 minutes until soft.

two Meanwhile, cook the beans in boiling water for about 3 minutes or until tender. Drain.

three Mix together the lime rind and juice, chili, ginger, sugar, and cilantro in a small bowl.

four Drain the noodles and place in a large serving bowl. Add the cooked beans, pineapple, and dressing and toss together lightly before serving.

Preparation time 15 minutes   Cooking time 15 minutes   Total time 30 minutes   Serves 4

rice noodle pancakes with stir-fried vegetables

6 oz. dried wide rice noodles
1 green chili, seeded and sliced
1 in. piece of fresh ginger, peeled and grated
3 tbsp. chopped cilantro
2 tsp. all-purpose flour
2 tsp. oil, plus extra for pan-frying

Stir-fried vegetables
4 oz. broccoli
2 tbsp. peanut or vegetable oil
1 small onion, sliced
1 red bell pepper, cored, seeded, and sliced
1 yellow or orange bell pepper, cored, seeded, and sliced
4 oz. sugarsnap peas, halved lengthwise
6 tbsp. hoisin sauce
1 tbsp. lime juice
salt and pepper

one Cook the noodles in lightly salted boiling water for 3 minutes or until tender. Drain well. Transfer to a bowl, then add the chili, ginger, cilantro, flour, and the 2 tsp. oil and mix well. Set aside.

two Thinly slice the broccoli stalks and cut the florets into small pieces. Cook the stalks in boiling water for 30 seconds, add the florets, and cook for 30 seconds more. Drain.

three Heat the peanut or vegetable oil in a wok or large frying pan, add the onion, and stir-fry for 2 minutes. Add the peppers and stir-fry for 3 minutes until softened but still retaining texture. Stir in the cooked broccoli, sugarsnap peas, hoisin sauce, and lime juice, season to taste with salt and pepper, and set aside.

four Heat some oil in a frying pan to a depth of ½ inch. Place 4 large, separate spoonfuls of the noodles (half the mixture) in the oil. Pan-fry for about 5 minutes until crisp and lightly colored. Drain the pancakes on paper towels. Keep warm while cooking the remaining noodle mixture.

five Heat the vegetables through for 1 minute in the wok or frying pan. Place 2 pancakes on each of 4 serving plates and pile the stir-fried vegetables on top.

Preparation time 5 minutes   Cooking time 15 minutes   Total time 20 minutes   Serves 3–4

crispy fried pasta cake

8 oz. capellini
4 tbsp. olive oil
2 onions, chopped
3 garlic cloves, crushed
½ cup pine nuts
3 oz. sun-dried tomatoes in oil, drained and finely shredded
3 oz. Parmesan cheese, grated
5 eggs, lightly beaten
4 tbsp. heavy cream
salt and pepper

one Cook the pasta in plenty of lightly salted boiling water for about 2 minutes or until only just tender. Drain.

two Meanwhile, heat 2 tbsp. of the oil in a heavy-bottomed frying pan. Add the onions, garlic, and pine nuts and sauté gently for 5 minutes until golden.

three Place the drained pasta in a bowl and add the onion mixture, sun-dried tomatoes, Parmesan, eggs, and cream. Season with salt and pepper and mix together thoroughly.

four Wipe out the pan and heat the remaining oil. When hot, add the pasta mixture, spreading it to the edges of the pan. Cook over moderate heat for about 5 minutes or until set and the underside looks golden when lifted with a spatula.

five Carefully invert the pasta on to a baking sheet or flat plate, then slide it back into the pan to cook the other side. Serve in wedges with a mixed salad.

beans & legumes

Simply opening a can
of beans, lentils, or other
legumes provides the
vegetarian cook with
one of the most versatile
vehicles for quick and
easy main meals. Use
them purely as a base
ingredient, letting the
highly flavored additions
of garlic, spices, herbs,
and aromatics transform
them into culinary
delights.

Preparation time 15 minutes Cooking time 10 minutes Total time 25 minutes Serves 4

nut koftas with minted yogurt

5–6 tbsp. peanut or vegetable oil
1 onion, chopped
½ tsp. crushed chili flakes
2 garlic cloves, coarsely chopped
1 tbsp. medium curry paste
14 oz. can cranberry or cannellini beans, rinsed and drained
1 cup ground almonds
⅓ cup chopped honey-roasted or salted almonds
1 small egg
7 oz. yogurt
2 tbsp. chopped mint
1 tbsp. lemon juice
salt and pepper
warm naan bread, to serve
mint sprigs, to garnish

one Soak 8 bamboo skewers in hot water while preparing the koftas. Alternatively, use metal skewers, which do not require presoaking.
Heat 3 tbsp. of the oil in a frying pan, add the onion and sauté for 4 minutes. Add the chili flakes, garlic, and curry paste and sauté for 1 minute.

two Transfer to a food processor or blender with the beans, ground almonds, chopped almonds, egg, and a little salt and pepper and process until the mixture starts to bind together.

three Using lightly floured hands, take about one-eighth of the mixture and mold around a skewer, forming it into a sausage about 1 inch thick. Make 7 more koftas in the same way.

four Place on a foil-lined broiler pan and brush with another tbsp. of the oil. Broil under a preheated moderate broiler for about 5 minutes, until golden, turning once.

five Meanwhile, mix together the yogurt and mint in a small serving bowl and season to taste with salt and pepper. In a separate bowl, mix together the remaining oil, lemon juice, and a little salt and pepper.

six Brush the koftas with the lemon dressing and serve with the yogurt dressing on warm naan bread garnished with mint sprigs.

Preparation time 3 minutes Total time 3 minutes Serves 4

garlic, herb, and bean pâté

14 oz. can flageolet beans, rinsed and drained
4 oz. cream cheese
2 garlic cloves, chopped
3 tbsp. Pesto (see page 9)
2 scallions, chopped
salt and pepper
chopped flat leaf parsley, to garnish

When you have only got a few minutes to put together a snack or starter, this recipe offers the ideal solution. Serve with a green salad and some warm, interesting bread or crackers.

one Place the beans, cream cheese, garlic, and pesto in a food processor or blender and process until combined.

two Add the scallions and salt and pepper and process for 10 seconds. Turn into a serving dish and chill until ready to serve. Serve scattered with parsley.

Preparation time 5 minutes Cooking time 25 minutes Total time 30 minutes Serves 4

braised lentils with mushrooms and gremolata

2 tbsp. butter
1 onion, chopped
2 celery stalks, sliced
2 carrots, sliced
6 oz. Puy lentils, rinsed
2 cups Vegetable Stock (see page 9)
1 cup dry white wine
2 bay leaves
2 tbsp. chopped thyme
3 tbsp. extra virgin olive oil
11 oz. mushrooms, sliced
salt and pepper

Gremolata
2 tbsp. chopped parsley
finely grated rind of 1 lemon
2 garlic cloves, chopped

Gremolata is simply a blend of chopped garlic, parsley, and lemon rind, which gives a delicious lift to soups and stews. Simply sprinkle it over before serving.

one Melt the butter in a saucepan and sauté the onion, celery, and carrots for 3 minutes. Add the lentils, stock, wine, herbs, and a little salt and pepper. Bring to a boil, then reduce the heat and simmer gently, uncovered, for about 20 minutes or until the lentils are tender.

two Meanwhile, mix together the ingredients for the gremolata.

three Heat the oil in a frying pan. Add the mushrooms and sauté quickly for about 2 minutes until golden. Season lightly with salt and pepper.

four Spoon the lentils on to serving plates, top with the mushrooms, and serve scattered with the gremolata.

Preparation time 8 minutes Cooking time 20 minutes Total time 28 minutes Serves 4

black bean and cabbage stew

4 tbsp. olive oil
1 large onion, chopped
1 leek, chopped
3 garlic cloves, sliced
1 tbsp. paprika
2 tbsp. chopped marjoram or thyme
1¼ lb. potatoes, cut into small chunks
14 oz. can black beans or black-eyed beans, rinsed and drained
3½ cups Vegetable Stock (see page 9)
6 oz. cabbage or scallions, shredded
salt and pepper
crusty bread, to serve

one Heat the oil in a large saucepan. Add the onion and leek and sauté gently for 3 minutes. Add the garlic and paprika and sauté for 2 minutes.

two Add the marjoram or thyme, potatoes, beans, and stock and bring to a boil. Reduce the heat, cover, and simmer gently for about 10 minutes until the potatoes have softened.

three Add the cabbage or scallions and season to taste with salt and pepper. Simmer for 5 minutes longer and serve with crusty bread.

red lentil dal with okra

1 onion, chopped
8 oz. red split lentils, rinsed and drained
1 tsp. ground turmeric
1 green chili, seeded and sliced
2 tbsp. tomato purée
3 cups Vegetable Stock (see page 9)
2 tbsp. creamed coconut
2 tbsp. peanut or vegetable oil
8 oz. okra, trimmed and halved crossways
2 tsp. cumin seeds
1 tbsp. mustard seeds
2 tsp. black onion seeds
2 garlic cloves, chopped
6 curry leaves (optional)
salt and pepper

Red lentils cook much faster than many legumes and do not need presoaking, making them a perfect choice for quick and easy cooking. Serve this spicy dish with naan or paratha bread and mango chutney to complete the meal.

one Place the onion, lentils, turmeric, chili, tomato purée, stock, and creamed coconut in a saucepan. Bring to a boil, then reduce the heat and simmer gently, uncovered, for 15 minutes or until thickened and pulpy. Stir frequently.

two Meanwhile, heat the oil in a frying pan. Add the okra, cumin seeds, mustard seeds, black onion seeds, garlic, and curry leaves, if using, and sauté gently for about 5 minutes until the okra is tender.

three Season the lentil dal to taste with salt and pepper and spoon on to serving plates. Serve topped with the spiced okra.

Preparation time 5 minutes   Cooking time 7 minutes   Total time 12 minutes   Serves 2

chickpea purée with eggs and spiced oil

14 oz. can chickpeas, rinsed and drained
3 garlic cloves, sliced
4 tbsp. tahini
4 tbsp. milk
5 tbsp. olive oil
4 tsp. lemon juice
2 eggs
½ tsp. each of cumin, coriander, and fennel seeds, lightly crushed
1 tsp. sesame seeds
¼ tsp. chili flakes
good pinch of ground turmeric
salt and pepper
cilantro leaves, to garnish

Smooth chickpea purée, topped with fried eggs and spicy oil, makes a great snack at any time of the day. Serve any leftover purée just as you would hummus, with warm pita bread.

one Place the chickpeas in a food processor or blender with the garlic, tahini, milk, 2 tbsp. of the oil, and 3 tsp. of the lemon juice. Season to taste with salt and pepper and process until smooth, scraping the mixture from around the sides of the bowl halfway through. Transfer to a small heavy-bottomed saucepan and heat through gently for about 3 minutes while preparing the eggs.

two Heat another tbsp. of the oil in a small frying pan and fry the eggs. Pile the chickpea purée on to serving plates and top each mound with an egg.

three Add the remaining oil and spices to the pan and heat through gently for 1 minute. Season lightly with salt and pepper and stir in the remaining lemon juice. Pour over the eggs and serve garnished with cilantro leaves.

Preparation time 8 minutes   Cooking time 22 minutes   Total time 30   Serves 4

red beans with
coconut and cashews

3 tbsp. peanut or vegetable oil
2 onions, chopped
2 small carrots, thinly sliced
3 garlic cloves, crushed
1 red bell pepper, cored, seeded, and chopped
2 bay leaves
1 tbsp. paprika
3 tbsp. tomato purée
14 oz. can coconut milk
7 oz. canned chopped tomatoes
½ cup Vegetable Stock (see page 9)
14 oz. can red kidney beans, rinsed and drained
½ cup unsalted, shelled cashew nuts, toasted
small handful of cilantro, coarsely chopped
salt and pepper
boiled brown or white rice, to serve

one Heat the oil in a large saucepan. Add the onions and carrots and sauté for 3 minutes. Add the garlic, pepper, and bay leaves and sauté for 5 minutes or until the vegetables are soft and well browned.

two Stir in the paprika, tomato purée, coconut milk, tomatoes, stock, and beans and bring to a boil. Reduce the heat and simmer, uncovered, for 12 minutes or until the vegetables are tender.

three Stir in the cashew nuts and cilantro, season to taste with salt and pepper, and heat through for 2 minutes. Serve with rice.

Preparation time 5 minutes   Cooking time 25 minutes   Total time 30 minutes   Serves 2–3

cannellini beans on toast

2 tbsp. peanut or vegetable oil
1 onion, chopped
1 celery stalk, thinly sliced
1 tsp. cornstarch
14 oz. can cannellini beans
8 oz. canned chopped tomatoes
1 cup Vegetable Stock (see page 9)
1 tbsp. coarse grain mustard
1 tbsp. molasses
1 tbsp. tomato ketchup
1 tbsp. Worcestershire sauce
salt and pepper
toasted chunky bread, to serve

This is a deliciously quick and easy version of Boston baked beans, on which the infamous commercial variety are based. Slightly spicy and sweet, it is comfort food at its best.

one Heat the oil in a saucepan and sauté the onion and celery for 5 minutes until golden. Blend the cornstarch with 2 tbsp. water and add to the pan with the remaining ingredients.

two Bring to a boil, reduce the heat slightly and cook, uncovered, for about 20 minutes, stirring frequently, until the mixture is thickened and pulpy. Pile on toast to serve.

Preparation time 15 minutes   Cooking time 6 minutes   Total time 21 minutes   Serves 4

chili, cheese, and corn cakes

4 oz. frozen corn, thawed
7 oz. can lima beans, rinsed and drained
¾ cup semolina or cornmeal
4 oz. Cheddar cheese, grated
½ tsp. dried chili flakes
4 tbsp. mango chutney
1 egg
oil, for pan-frying
salt and pepper

These little corn cakes make a welcome change from bread for serving with salads or as a snack. If you do not want to cook them all at once, the shaped cakes can be chilled for up to two days.

one Place the corn and beans in a food processor or blender and process until chopped into very small pieces, or mash with a fork in a bowl. Transfer to a bowl, if necessary, and add the semolina or cornmeal, cheese, and chili flakes.

two Chop any large pieces of chutney. Add to the bowl with the egg and mix until it forms a dough.

three Using lightly floured hands, shape the mixture into 12 balls, then flatten into cakes. Heat a little oil in a frying pan, add the cakes and sauté gently for about 3 minutes on each side until golden. Drain on paper towels and serve warm.

Preparation time 10 minutes   Cooking time 10 minutes   Total time 20 minutes   Serves 4

red bean and pepper cakes with lemon mayonnaise

3 oz. green beans, coarsely chopped
2 tbsp. peanut or vegetable oil
1 red bell pepper, cored, seeded, and diced
4 garlic cloves, crushed
2 tsp. mild chili powder
14 oz. can red kidney beans, rinsed and drained
¾ cup fresh white breadcrumbs
1 egg yolk
oil, for pan-frying

Lemon mayonnaise
4 tbsp. mayonnaise
finely grated rind of 1 lemon
1 tsp. lemon juice
salt and pepper

Pack these crisp bean cakes into warm pita bread and serve with salad for a fairly substantial lunch or supper dish. Any unbaked cakes will keep in the refrigerator, covered with waxed paper, for a day or so.

one Blanch the green beans in boiling water for 1–2 minutes until softened. Drain.

two Meanwhile, heat the peanut or vegetable oil in a frying pan and sauté the pepper, garlic, and chili powder for 2 minutes.

three Transfer the mixture to a food processor or blender and add the red kidney beans, breadcrumbs, and egg yolk. Process very briefly until the ingredients are coarsely chopped. Add the drained green beans and season to taste with salt and pepper and process until the ingredients are just combined.

four Turn the mixture into a bowl and divide into 8 portions. Using lightly floured hands, shape the portions into little cakes.

five Mix the mayonnaise with the lemon rind and juice, and season to taste with salt and pepper.

six Heat the oil for frying in a large frying pan and pan-fry the cakes for about 3 minutes on each side until crisp and golden. Serve with the lemon mayonnaise.

brown beans with lemon, parsley, and egg dressing

4 garlic cloves, crushed
1 tsp. cumin seeds
½ bunch of scallions, thinly sliced
small handful of parsley, chopped
1 tbsp. lemon juice
2 tsp. harissa paste
4 tbsp. olive oil
14 oz. can brown beans, rinsed and drained
1 small pickled cucumber, coarsely chopped
2 hard-boiled eggs, coarsely chopped
salt and pepper
whole-grain bread, to serve

This dish makes a great starter or side salad. Health food stores and delicatessens are most likely to stock brown beans. The canned variety tend to be large, flattish, and quite bland, hence the spiced, tangy dressing. Red kidney beans or lima beans make a good substitute.

one Mix together the garlic, cumin seeds, scallions, parsley, lemon juice, harrisa, and oil in a large bowl.

two Add the beans, cucumber, and eggs, and season to taste with salt and pepper. Toss together gently and transfer to the oiled bowl. Serve with whole-grain bread.

bean and beer casserole with baby dumplings

4 tbsp. peanut or vegetable oil
1 onion, sliced
1 celery stalk, thinly sliced
1 parsnip, sliced
14 oz. can mixed beans, rinsed and drained
14 oz. can baked beans
1 cup Guinness or other stout
1 cup Vegetable Stock (see page 9)
4 tbsp. coarsely chopped herbs, such as rosemary, marjoram, thyme
1¼ cup. self-rising flour
⅓ cup vegetable shortening
2 tbsp. coarse grain mustard
salt and pepper

one Heat the oil in a large saucepan or flameproof casserole and sauté the onion, celery, and parsnip for 3 minutes. Add the mixed beans, baked beans, beer, stock, and 3 tbsp. of the herbs. Bring to a boil and let the mixture bubble, uncovered, for 8–10 minutes or until slightly thickened.

two Meanwhile, mix the flour, shortening, mustard, remaining herbs, and a little salt and pepper in a bowl with 8–9 tbsp. cold water to make a soft dough.

three Evenly distribute 8 spoonfuls of the dough in the casserole and cover the pan or dish. Cook for 10 minutes more or until the dumplings are light and fluffy. Serve immediately.

rice

Rice is the staple ingredient of so many countries worldwide that it offers a fabulous choice of interesting dishes for the vegetarian cook. Although some varieties take longer to cook, there are still plenty of easy options to offer, including sweet, aromatic oriental dishes, spicy Middle Eastern-style pilafs, and creamy, comforting Italian risottos.

Preparation time 10 minutes Cooking time 20 minutes Total time 30 minutes Serves 4

chestnut risotto cakes

½ oz. dried porcini mushrooms
1 tbsp. olive oil
1 cup arborio rice
2¼ cups hot Vegetable Stock (see page 9)
2 tbsp. butter
1 onion, chopped
3 garlic cloves, crushed
7 oz. cooked, peeled chestnuts, chopped
3 oz. Parmesan cheese, grated
1 egg, lightly beaten
2 oz. cornmeal
oil, for pan-frying
salt and pepper
dressed leafy green salad, to serve

These delicious little cakes are crisp on the outside yet moist and risotto-like in the center. If you do not need the full quantity, freeze the shaped but uncooked mixture for a later date.

one Place the dried mushrooms in a bowl and cover with boiling water. Let stand while preparing the rice.

two Heat the olive oil in a saucepan. Add the rice and cook, stirring, for 1 minute. Add the hot stock and bring to a boil. Reduce the heat, partially cover, and simmer for about 12–15 minutes, stirring frequently, until the rice is tender and the stock is absorbed. Transfer to a bowl.

three Meanwhile, melt the butter in a saucepan. Add the onion and garlic and sauté gently for 2 minutes. Drain and chop the mushrooms, then add to the rice with the onion mixture, chestnuts, Parmesan, and egg. Stir until combined and season lightly with salt and pepper.

four Divide the mixture into 12 portions. Pat each portion into a cake and roll in the cornmeal. Heat the oil for frying and pan-fry the cakes for 2 minutes on each side or until golden. Serve immediately with a dressed leafy green salad.

Preparation time 5 minutes Cooking time 25 minutes Total time 30 minutes Serves 4

fava bean, lemon, and parmesan risotto

1 tbsp. butter
2 tbsp. olive oil
1 onion, chopped
2 garlic cloves, crushed
1½ cups arborio rice
½ cup dry white wine
4 cups hot Vegetable Stock (see page 9)
5 oz. fresh or frozen fava beans
2 oz. Parmesan cheese, grated, plus extra to serve
finely grated rind and juice of 1 lemon
salt and pepper

one Melt the butter with the oil in a large, heavy-bottomed saucepan. Add the onion and garlic and sauté gently for 3 minutes. Add the rice and cook for 1 minute, stirring.

two Add the wine and cook, stirring, until the wine is absorbed. Add a little stock and cook, stirring, until almost absorbed. Continue in the same way, gradually adding more stock, until half the stock is used. Stir in the beans.

three Gradually add the remaining stock until the mixture is thickened and creamy but still retaining a little bite. This will take 15–18 minutes. Stir in the Parmesan, lemon rind and juice, and season to taste with salt and pepper. Turn on to serving plates and serve with extra Parmesan cheese.

Preparation time 5 minutes Cooking time 25 minutes Total time 30 minutes Serves 4

red rice and pepper pilaf

1 cup Camargue red rice
2 cups hot Vegetable Stock (see page 9)
3 tbsp. olive oil
1 large red onion, chopped
2 tbsp. paprika
3 garlic cloves, crushed
1 tsp. saffron threads
2 red bell peppers, cored, seeded, and sliced
finely grated rind of 1 lemon,
2 tsp. lemon juice
4 tomatoes, coarsely chopped
small handful of flat leaf parsley, coarsely chopped, plus extra to garnish
½ cup pitted black olives
salt and pepper

one Place the rice, hot stock, and 2 cups boiling water in a large saucepan. bring to a boil, cover and cook for 25 minutes until tender, stirring frequently.

two Meanwhile, heat the oil in a saucepan or frying pan. Add the onion and sauté gently for 3 minutes. Add the paprika, garlic, saffron, and peppers and sauté gently for 5 minutes.

three Stir in the lemon rind and juice, tomatoes, and parsley and cook gently, uncovered, for 5 minutes.

four Drain the rice and add to the pan with the olives and season to taste with salt and pepper. Toss together and serve scattered with extra parsley.

Preparation time 10 minutes Cooking time 15 minutes Total time 25 minutes Serves 4

japanese rice with nori

1¼ cups Japanese sushi or glutinous rice
1¾ cups water
2 tbsp. black or white sesame seeds
1 tsp. coarse salt
1 tbsp. peanut or vegetable oil
2 eggs, beaten
4 scallions, finely sliced
1 red chili, seeded and sliced
4 tbsp. seasoned rice vinegar
2 tsp. sugar
1 tbsp. light soy sauce
1 oz. pickled Japanese ginger
2 sheets of roasted nori seaweed

one Place the rice in a heavy-bottomed saucepan with 1¾ cups water. Bring to a boil, then reduce the heat and simmer, uncovered, for about 5 minutes or until all the water is absorbed. Cover the pan and cook for 5 minutes longer, until the rice is cooked.

two Meanwhile, place the sesame seeds in a small frying pan with the salt and heat gently for about 2 minutes until the seeds are lightly toasted. Remove from the pan and set aside.

three Heat the oil in the pan, add the beaten eggs, and cook gently until just firm. Slide the omelette on to a plate, roll up, and cut across into shreds.

four Transfer the cooked rice to a bowl and stir in the spring onions, chili, rice vinegar, sugar, soy sauce, ginger, and half the toasted sesame seeds. Crumble 1 sheet of nori over the rice and stir in with the omelette shreds.

five Transfer to a serving dish. Crumble the remaining nori over the rice and scatter with the remaining toasted sesame seeds.

Preparation time 7 minutes Cooking time 23 minutes Total time 30 minutes Serves 4

spiced pilaf with pickled walnuts

3 tbsp. olive oil
1 large onion, chopped
4 garlic cloves, sliced
¼ tsp. ground allspice
½ cup pine nuts
2 tsp. ground ginger
1 cup long-grain rice
1 tsp. saffron threads
2 cups Vegetable Stock (see page 9)
½ cup pickled walnuts, coarsely chopped
½ cup dried apricots, sliced
4 tbsp. coarsely chopped cilantro
salt and pepper
yogurt, to serve

one Heat the oil in a large, heavy-bottomed frying pan. Add the onion, garlic, allspice, pine nuts, and ginger and sauté gently for 5 minutes.

two Add the rice and cook for 1 minute, stirring. Add the saffron and stock and bring to a boil. Reduce the heat, partially cover, and simmer gently for 10–15 minutes until the rice is tender, adding a little more stock if the mixture becomes too dry.

three Add the pickled walnuts, apricots, and cilantro, and season to taste with salt and pepper. Heat through for 2 minutes, then serve with yogurt.

Preparation time 5 minutes Cooking time 25 minutes Total time 30 minutes Serves 4

sage and walnut risotto with a cheese crust

2 tbsp. butter
1 onion, chopped
1½ cups arborio rice
4½ cups hot Vegetable Stock (see page 9)
2 tbsp. chopped sage
½ cup walnuts, coarsely chopped
8 oz. brie, thinly sliced
salt and pepper
leafy green salad, to serve

one Melt the butter in a large, heavy-bottomed saucepan. Add the onion and sauté for 2 minutes. Add the rice and sauté for 1 minute, stirring.

two Add 2 ladlefuls of the stock and cook, stirring, until almost absorbed. Add a little more stock and continue cooking, stirring, until almost absorbed. Continue in the same way until all the stock is used and the rice is creamy but still retaining a little bite. This will take 15–18 minutes.

three Stir in the sage and walnuts, and season to taste with salt and pepper. Transfer to a shallow flameproof serving dish and cover with the slices of brie. Cook under a preheated hot grill for about 3 minutes or until the cheese has melted. Serve with a leafy green salad.

Preparation time 5 minutes Cooking time 15 minutes Total time 20 minutes Serves 4

kedgeree with artichokes and rosemary butter

1 cup basmati rice
2 tbsp. butter, melted
1 tbsp. chopped rosemary
1 tbsp. chopped chives
1 tbsp. lime juice
2 tbsp. olive oil
1 onion, chopped
1 tsp. coriander seeds, crushed
1 tsp. fennel seeds, crushed
14 oz. can artichoke hearts, rinsed, drained and halved
6 hard-boiled eggs, cut into wedges
salt and pepper
lime wedges, to garnish

one Cook the rice in plenty of lightly salted boiling water for about 10 minutes or until just tender.

two Meanwhile, mix together the melted butter, chopped herbs, and lime juice, and season with salt and pepper.

three Heat the oil in a frying pan. Add the onion and spices and sauté gently for 5 minutes. Drain the rice and add to the pan with the artichoke hearts, season to taste with salt and pepper, and heat through gently for 1 minute. Lightly stir in the eggs.

four Transfer to serving plates and pour over the herb butter. Serve garnished with lime wedges.

coconut rice with peanut sauce

10 oz. jasmine or Thai fragrant rice
3 oz. creamed coconut
½ tsp. dried chili flakes
1 tsp. sugar
small handful of cilantro, chopped
11 inch lengths of banana leaf, washed
1 lime
1 papaya, peeled, seeded, and sliced
4 scallions, shredded lengthwise
¾ cup roasted, salted cashew nuts
salt and pepper

Sauce
½ small onion, finely chopped
1 lemon grass stalk, finely sliced
4 tbsp. peanut butter
1 tbsp. dark brown sugar
2 tbsp. creamed coconut
2 tbsp. soy sauce

Cooking food in banana-leaf packets keeps its flavor and moisture intact and makes an exotic presentation if you are entertaining. If not, simply wrap the rice in nonstick baking parchment or foil for heating through.

one Place the rice in a saucepan with the creamed coconut and ¾ cup water, bring to a boil, then reduce the heat, and simmer gently, stirring frequently, for about 5 minutes until the water is almost absorbed and the mixture is creamy. Remove from the heat and stir in the chili flakes, sugar, and cilantro. Season to taste with salt and pepper.

two Spoon the mixture on to the centers of the banana leaves. Fold over the sides to enclose the rice, then tuck the ends under to form packets. Place on a baking sheet and bake in a preheated 425°F oven for about 5 minutes or until the leaves have browned.

three Meanwhile, place the ingredients for the sauce in a small saucepan and heat through gently until thickened, stirring frequently.

four Using a paring knife, peel fine strips of rind from the lime. Cut away the remaining white skin and discard, then cut between the membranes to remove the segments.

five Open the parcels and add the papaya, scallions, cashew nuts, lime segments, and rind. Serve with the sauce.

spiced vegetable biryani

1¼ cups basmati rice
3 tbsp. peanut or vegetable oil
1 large onion, chopped
2 inch piece of fresh ginger, peeled and grated
2 garlic cloves, chopped
2 tsp. cumin seeds
1 tsp. ground turmeric
½ tsp. dried chili flakes
2½ cups Vegetable Stock (see page 9)
7 oz. green beans
8 oz. cauliflower florets
1 tbsp. garam masala
salt and pepper

one Cook the rice in plenty of boiling water for about 10 minutes or until just tender.

two Meanwhile, heat the oil in a large saucepan. Add the onion, ginger, garlic, cumin seeds, turmeric, and chili flakes and sauté gently for 6 minutes.

three Add the stock and bring to a boil. Add the beans and cauliflower, reduce the heat, and simmer for 10 minutes, uncovered, until the vegetables are tender, stirring frequently.

four Drain the rice and add to the pan with the garam masala, season to taste with salt and pepper, and heat through for 2 minutes before serving.

Preparation time 5 minutes Cooking time 25 minutes Total time 30 minutes Serves 4

beet risotto with horseradish and mixed greens

4 tbsp. olive oil
1 large red onion, chopped
3 garlic cloves, crushed
2 cups risotto rice
4½ cups hot Vegetable Stock (see page 9)
14 oz. cooked beets, finely diced
4 tbsp. coarsely chopped dill
1–2 tbsp. freshly grated horseradish or 1 tbsp. hot horseradish from a jar
½ cup salted macadamia nuts or almonds
salt and pepper
mixed salad greens, to serve

This risotto makes an impressive main course for 4 people, but will also serve 6–8 as a colorful starter. If you can find fresh horseradish, use it in place of the bottled variety. The flavor is far superior, but beware of its heat intensity which can be anything from harmlessly mild to hot and fiery, depending on its freshness.

one Heat the oil in a large, heavy-bottomed saucepan. Add the onion and garlic and sauté gently for 3 minutes. Add the rice and cook for 1 minute, stirring.

two Add 2 ladlefuls of the stock and cook, stirring frequently, until almost absorbed. Add a little more stock and continue cooking, stirring frequently, until almost absorbed. Continue in the same way until all the stock is used and the rice is creamy but still retaining a little bite. This will take about 20 minutes.

three Stir in the beets, dill, horseradish, and nuts and heat through gently for 1 minute. Spoon on to serving plates and serve scattered with mixed salad greens.

Preparation time 5 minutes Cooking time 25 minutes Total time 30 minutes Serves 4

lemon rice with feta and charbroiled peppers

3 tbsp. olive oil
1 onion, sliced
3 garlic cloves, crushed
1 small lemon, sliced
1 cup long-grain rice
2 cups Vegetable Stock (see page 9)
1 tbsp. chopped rosemary
1 large zucchini
2 red bell peppers, cored, seeded, and cut into 8 pieces
1 yellow bell pepper, cored, seeded, and cut into 8 pieces
7 oz. feta cheese, diced
salt and pepper

one Heat 2 tbsp. of the oil in a heavy-bottomed saucepan. Add the onion and sauté quickly for 3 minutes. Add the garlic and lemon slices and sauté for 2 minutes. Add the rice, stock, and rosemary and bring to a boil. Reduce the heat slightly, partially cover, and cook for about 15 minutes or until the rice is just tender and the stock is absorbed. Add a little more stock or water if the mixture becomes too dry.

two Cut the zucchini diagonally into long thin slices. Heat the remaining oil in a griddle or large frying pan. Add the zucchini slices and peppers and cook quickly for 5 minutes until colored, turning the vegetables, and pressing the peppers down on to the pan with a spatula as they soften.

three Add the cooked vegetables to the rice, fold in gently with the feta, and season to taste with salt and pepper. Heat through for 1 minute before serving.

pizza & bread

Made using a quick and
simple bread crust, lavishly
topped pizzas are surprisingly
quick to prepare and create
an enduringly appealing lunch
or dinner dish. Ready-made
breads, both yeast-risen and
flat, offer ultra-easy meal
solutions, providing instant
crusts for a variety of
exciting vegetarian fillings
and toppings.

Preparation time 12 minutes   Cooking time 15 minutes   Total time 27 minutes   Serves 4

spinach, onion, and cream cheese pizza

2 cups self-rising flour
3 tbsp. olive oil
1 teaspoon salt

Topping
3½ oz. full-fat soft cheese
3½ oz. crème fraîche
2 tsp. chopped rosemary
3 tbsp. olive oil
1 large onion, finely sliced
12 oz. young spinach
salt and pepper

one Grease a large baking sheet. Place the flour in a bowl with the oil and salt. Add 7 tbsp. water and mix to a soft dough, adding a little more water if the dough is too dry. Roll out on a floured surface into a round about 11 inches in diameter. Place on the prepared baking sheet and bake in a preheated 450°F oven for 5 minutes or until a crust has formed.

two For the topping, beat together the cream cheese, crème fraîche, rosemary, and a little salt and pepper.

three Heat the oil in a frying pan and sauté the onion for 3–4 minutes until softened. Add the spinach and a little salt and pepper and cook, stirring, for about 1 minute or until the spinach has just wilted.

four Pile the spinach on to the pizza crust, spreading to within ½ inch of the edge. Place spoonfuls of the cheese mixture over the spinach. Bake 8 more minutes or until cheese turn golden.

spinach and egg muffins with mustard hollandaise

7 oz. baby spinach
plenty of freshly ground nutmeg
1 tbsp. lemon juice
2 egg yolks
1 tbsp. coarse grain mustard
3 tbsp. lightly salted butter, diced
4 English muffins, split
1 tbsp. vinegar
4 eggs

one Place the spinach and nutmeg in a saucepan and add 1 tbsp. water. Set aside while making the sauce.

two Place the lemon juice, egg yolks, and mustard in a heatproof bowl over a pan of gently simmering water. Add a piece of the butter and whisk until the butter has melted into the sauce. Continue whisking in the butter, a piece at a time, until the sauce is thickened and smooth. This takes about 5 minutes. If the sauce becomes too thick, whisk in a tablespoonful of hot water. Keep the sauce warm over the simmering water until ready to use.

three Toast the English muffins and keep warm. Place the vinegar in a saucepan with plenty of hot water, bring to a boil and poach the eggs. Cover the spinach pan with a lid and cook for about 1 minute until the spinach has wilted.

four Transfer the English muffins to serving plates, pile them up with the spinach, then the poached eggs, and finally the sauce. Serve immediately.

goat cheese, onion, and pine nut bruschetta

5 tbsp. olive oil
1 small red onion, chopped
3 tbsp. pine nuts
4 slices Italian bread
1 garlic clove, crushed
2 tbsp. chopped flat leaf parsley
5 oz. firm goat cheese, thinly sliced

one Heat 2 tbsp. of the oil in a frying pan, add the onion and pine nuts, and sauté for 3 minutes until softened.

two Toast one side of the bread under a preheated moderate broiler until golden. Mix together the garlic, parsley, and remaining oil in a bowl. Turn the bread over and spread with the garlic mixture. Broil until pale golden.

three Lay the goat cheese and onion mixture over the toast, increase the heat, and broil for 2 minutes longer. Serve warm.

Preparation time 10 minutes Cooking time 20 minutes Total time 30 minutes Serves 4

tomato, artichoke, and mozzarella pizza

2 cups self-rising flour
3 tbsp. oil
1 tsp. salt
2 tbsp. sun-dried tomato paste

Topping
1 tbsp. sun-dried tomato paste
2 large, mild red or green chilies, halved and seeded
3 tbsp. chopped mixed herbs, such as
parsley, oregano, rosemary, chives
2 oz. sun-dried tomatoes in oil, drained and sliced
5 oz. baby artichokes in oil, drained
2 plum tomatoes, cut into quarters
5 oz. mozzarella cheese, sliced
½ cup black olives
salt and pepper

Homemade pizzas look and taste infinitely better than most store-bought ones and are certainly a much better value for the money. If you are unable to find the large, really mild chilies, use strips of red bell pepper instead or scatter the pizza with a finely sliced hot chili.

one Grease a large baking sheet. Place the flour in a bowl with the oil, salt, and sun-dried tomato paste. Add 7 tbsp. water and mix to a soft dough, adding a little more water if necessary.

two Roll out the dough on a lightly floured surface to a round about 11 inches in diameter. Place on the prepared baking sheet and bake in a preheated 450°F oven for 5 minutes.

three For the topping, spread the pizza crust to within ½ inch of the edge with the sun-dried tomato paste. Cut the chilies in half lengthwise again and scatter over the pizza with half the herbs, the sun-dried tomatoes, artichokes, tomatoes, cheese, and olives. Scatter the remaining herbs on top and season lightly with salt and pepper. Return to the oven and bake for 10–15 minutes until the cheese has melted and the vegetables are beginning to color.

Preparation time 5 minutes Cooking time 5 minutes Total time 10 minutes Serves 2

tortilla wraps with refried beans and cilantro relish

8 oz. can refried beans
2 tbsp. chili sauce
2 red bell peppers, cored, seeded, and finely chopped
4 scallions, finely sliced
1 tsp. cumin seeds
finely grated rind and juice of 1 lime
1 tsp. sugar
½ oz. cilantro, chopped
4 tortillas
salt and pepper

one Place the beans in a small saucepan with the chili sauce and heat through gently for 3 minutes.

two Mix together in a bowl the peppers, scallions, cumin seeds, lime rind and juice, sugar, and cilantro. Season to taste with salt and pepper.

three Lightly toast the tortillas and spread with the refried beans. Spoon over the cilantro mixture and roll up the tortillas.

Preparation time 10 minutes Cooking time 8 minutes Total time 18 minutes Serves 4

cheddar burgers with cucumber salsa

7 oz. can lima beans, rinsed and drained
1 onion, finely chopped
1 carrot, grated
3½ oz. mature cheddar cheese, grated
1 cup breadcrumbs
1 egg
1 tsp. cumin seeds
oil, for pan-frying
4 round French rolls
salad, to serve

Salsa
½ small cucumber
2 tbsp. chopped cilantro
2 scallions, finely chopped
1 tbsp. lemon or lime juice
1 tsp. sugar
salt and pepper

one Place the lima beans in a bowl and lightly mash with a fork. Add the onion, carrot, cheese, breadcrumbs, egg, cumin seeds, and salt and pepper and mix until evenly combined.

two Using lightly floured hands, shape the mixture into 8 small flat cakes. Heat a little oil in a large frying pan and pan-fry the burgers for about 8 minutes, turning once, until crisp and golden.

three Meanwhile, for the salsa, halve the cucumber and scoop out the seeds. Finely chop the cucumber and toss in a bowl with the cilantro, scallions, lemon or lime juice, sugar, and a little salt and pepper.

four Split the rolls and make a sandwich with the burgers and salsa. Serve with salad.

Preparation time 10 minutes Cooking time 5 minutes Total time 15 minutes Serves 4

toasted goat cheese with sun-dried tomato pesto

4 chunky slices of walnut or
whole-grain bread
8 oz. goat cheese
leafy green salad, to serve

Sun-dried tomato pesto
4 oz. sun-dried tomatoes in oil, drained
4 tbsp. pine nuts
10 pitted black olives
2 garlic cloves, coarsely chopped
5 tbsp. olive oil
1 oz. Parmesan cheese, grated
salt and pepper

Sun-dried tomato pesto has all the vibrant flavor of the better-known basil version (see page 9), and serves equally as many uses. Try it spread on pizzas, tossed with pasta, or stirred into vegetable soups and stews.

one To make the pesto, place the sun-dried tomatoes in a food processor or blender with the pine nuts, olives, and garlic. Process until chopped.

two With the motor running, add the oil in a steady stream. Once combined, turn into a bowl and stir in the Parmesan and salt and pepper.

three Toast one side of the bread under a preheated moderate broiler. Turn the bread over and top with the goat cheese. Increase the heat and broil until the cheese is melting and golden. Transfer to serving plates and spoon over the pesto. Serve with a leafy green salad.

Preparation time 10 minutes Cooking time 10 minutes Total time 20 minutes Serves 2

tortillas with minted chili yogurt and eggplant

4 tbsp. olive oil
1 medium eggplant, thinly sliced
small handful of mint, chopped
small handful of parsley, chopped
2 tbsp. chopped chives
1 green chili, seeded and thinly sliced
7 oz. yogurt
2 tbsp. mayonnaise
2 large tortillas
3 inch length of cucumber, thinly sliced
salt and pepper
paprika, to garnish

one Heat the oil in a frying pan. Add the eggplant and sauté for about 10 minutes until golden. Drain and set aside to cool.

two Mix the herbs with the chili, yogurt, and mayonnaise in a bowl and season to taste with salt and pepper .

three Arrange the fried eggplant slices over the tortillas and spread with the yogurt mixture. Arrange the cucumber slices on top. Roll up each tortilla, sprinkle with paprika and serve.

pancakes & pastries

Whether made from batter or vegetables, pancakes can be classic or inventive, taking on a main meal role with an eclectic mix of tempting toppings and fillings to suit your tastes and moods. Extend the variety by using ready-made pastries, such as mouth-wateringly crisp phyllo and rich, golden puff pastry, for great results in just a few minutes.

Preparation time 10 minutes   Cooking time 10 minutes   Total time 20 minutes   Serves 4

phyllo, pesto, and mozzarella pockets

4 oz. phyllo pastry sheets
2 tbsp. butter, melted
3 tbsp. Sun-dried Tomato Pesto (see page 65)
8 oz. mozzarella cheese, drained and sliced
2 oz. Parmesan, grated
leafy green salad, to serve

Unfortunately, phyllo pastry sheets vary considerably in size, so bear this in mind when shaping it into pockets. As long as the cheese is wrapped in a double thickness of overlapping phyllo, it should not seep out during baking.

one Cut the phyllo pastry into sixteen 6 inch squares. Lay 8 squares on the surface and brush with a little melted butter. Cover each with a second square.

two Dot the pesto into the centers of the squares and spread slightly. Arrange the mozzarella and Parmesan over the pesto. Season lightly with salt and pepper.

three Bring two opposite sides of the pastry over the filling to enclose completely. Lightly brush with butter, then fold over the two open ends to make pockets. Place on a baking sheet with the ends on top.

four Brush with the remaining butter (melt a little more if necessary) and bake in a preheated oven, 400°F, for about 10 minutes or until golden. Serve warm with a leafy green salad.

Preparation time 8 minutes Cooking time 22 minutes Total time 30 minutes Serves 4

carrot and potato rosti

1½ lb. potatoes
8 oz. carrots
1 tbsp. butter
2 tbsp. olive oil
salt and pepper

Any recipe that incorporates both potatoes and frying is almost guaranteed to taste delicious. This fried potato and carrot cake can be served as an accompaniment or simply piled up with spinach and eggs, charbroiled vegetables, or diced cheese and tomatoes as a meal in itself.

one Cut the potatoes and carrots into chunks and cook in lightly salted boiling water for about 8 minutes or until softened but retaining texture. Drain and leave for 2 minutes.

two Coarsely grate the potatoes and carrots, either by hand or using a food processor. Transfer to a bowl and toss with a little salt and pepper.

three Melt the butter with the oil in a nonstick or heavy-bottomed frying pan. When very hot, add the vegetables and pack them down gently in an even layer. Reduce the heat slightly and pan-fry for 8–10 minutes until the underside looks golden when lifted with a spatula.

four To turn the rosti, invert it on to a baking sheet or flat plate, then slide it back into the pan. Sauté for 3–4 minutes longer. Serve cut into wedges.

Preparation time 10 minutes Cooking time 20 minutes Total time 30 minutes Serves 6

zucchini pancakes with swiss cheese and peppers

11 oz. zucchini
1½ cups plain flour
3 eggs
3 tbsp. butter, melted
½ cup milk
1 tbsp. chopped thyme
6 tbsp. olive oil
10 oz. eggplant, cut into small chunks
2 small red onions, sliced
2 red bell peppers, cored, seeded and sliced
13 oz. can chopped tomatoes
2 tbsp. balsamic vinegar
10 oz. Swiss cheese, thinly sliced
oil, for pan-frying
salt and pepper

These crisp little pancakes, topped with melting cheese and a ratatouille-style topping, make a thoroughly enjoyable starter, or increase the size of the pancakes and serve with a salad for a main course.

one Grate the zucchini. In a large bowl, beat together the flour, eggs, butter, milk, and thyme to make a smooth batter. Stir in the grated zucchini and season with salt and pepper.

two Heat the olive oil in a large, heavy-bottomed saucepan or frying pan. Add the eggplant and onions and sauté for about 5 minutes until turning golden. Add the peppers and continue frying quickly for about 3 minutes until the vegetables are lightly browned. Add the tomatoes, vinegar, and salt and pepper. Reduce the heat and simmer gently, uncovered, for 10 minutes while preparing the pancakes.

three Heat a little oil in a large frying pan. Add a tablespoonful of the pancake mixture to one side of the pan and spread to about 4 inches. Add as many more spoonfuls of the batter as the pan will contain and fry for about 2 minutes or until golden on the underside. Turn the pancakes and cook for 2 minutes longer. Drain on paper towels and transfer to a broiler pan. Cook the remainder of the pancakes (the mixture should make 12 total).

four Arrange the cheese slices over the pancakes and broil under a preheated hot broiler until the cheese is melting. Arrange 2 pancakes on each serving plate, overlapping them slightly. Pile the pepper sauce on top and serve warm.

cherry tomato tarts with pesto crème fraîche

2 tbsp. extra virgin olive oil
1 onion, finely chopped
12 oz. cherry tomatoes
2 garlic cloves, crushed
3 tbsp. sun-dried tomato paste
11 oz. puff pastry
beaten egg, to glaze
5 oz. crème fraîche
2 tbsp. Pesto (see page 9)
salt and pepper
basil leaves, to garnish

one Lightly grease a large baking sheet and sprinkle with water. Heat the oil in a frying pan, add the onion, and sauté for about 3 minutes until softened. Halve about 5 oz. of the tomatoes. Remove the pan from the heat, add the garlic and sun-dried tomato paste, then stir in all the tomatoes until lightly coated with the sauce.

two Roll out the pastry on a lightly floured surface and cut out four 5 inch rounds using a cutter or small bowl as a guide. Transfer to the prepared baking sheet and make a shallow cut ½ inch from the edge of each round using the tip of a sharp knife, to form a rim. Brush the rims with beaten egg. Pile the tomato mixture on to the centers of the pastries, making sure the mixture stays within the rims.

three Bake in a preheated oven, 425°F, for about 15 minutes until the pastry is puffed and golden.

four Meanwhile, lightly mix together the crème fraîche, pesto, and salt and pepper in a bowl so that the crème fraîche is streaked with the pesto.

five When cooked, transfer the tartlets to serving plates and spoon over the crème fraîche pesto. Serve scattered with basil leaves.

falafel cakes

14 oz. can chickpeas, rinsed and drained
1 onion, coarsely chopped
3 garlic cloves, coarsely chopped
2 tsp. cumin seeds
1 tsp. mild chili powder
2 tbsp. chopped mint
3 tbsp. chopped cilantro
½ cup breadcrumbs
oil, for pan-frying
salt and pepper

These tasty chickpea cakes, traditionally rolled into little balls and deep fried, make a great veggie supper served simply with a fresh, Greek-style salad.

one Place the chickpeas in a food processor or blender with the onion, garlic, spices, herbs, breadcrumbs, and a little salt and pepper. Blend briefly to make a chunky paste.

two Take teaspoonfuls of the mixture and flatten into cakes. Heat a ½ inch depth of oil in a frying pan and pan-fry half the falafel for about 3 minutes, turning once, until crisp and golden. Drain on paper towels and keep warm while cooking the remainder.

Preparation time 10 minutes Cooking time 16 minutes Total time 26 minutes Serves 4

minted pea cake with mozzarella, tomato, and basil

1 lb. potatoes
8 oz. peas
3 tbsp. chopped mint
1 egg, lightly beaten
10 oz. mozzarella, sliced
6 plum tomatoes, sliced
6 tbsp. extra virgin olive oil
1 tbsp. balsamic vinegar
small handful of basil leaves, shredded
2 tbsp. butter
salt and pepper

one Cut the potatoes into chunks and cook in lightly salted boiling water for about 8 minutes, until softened but still retaining their texture.

two Meanwhile, cook the peas in a separate pan of lightly salted boiling water for 2 minutes. Drain the peas and place in a bowl, then mash with a fork until broken up. Coarsely grate the potatoes and add to the bowl with the mint, beaten egg, and salt and pepper. Mix together until evenly combined.

three Arrange alternate overlapping slices of the cheese and tomatoes in a shallow flameproof dish and season lightly with salt and pepper. Mix 5 tbsp. of the olive oil with the vinegar and basil for the dressing.

four Melt the butter with the remaining oil in a heavy-bottomed frying pan. Add the potato and pea mixture and pack down gently in an even layer. Sauté over a moderate heat for about 5 minutes or until the underside looks crisp and golden when lifted with a spatula.

five To turn the pancake, invert it on to a baking sheet or flat plate, then slide it back into the pan and pan-fry for 3 minutes longer. While cooking, broil the cheese and tomatoes under a preheated hot broiler until the cheese starts to melt.

six Cut the pancake into wedges and transfer to serving plates. Pile the cheese and tomatoes on top and spoon over the dressing.

Preparation time 10 minutes Cooking time 20 minutes Total time 30 minutes Serves 4

camembert and shallot tarts

2 tbsp. butter
8 large shallots, each cut into 4 wedges
1 tbsp. chopped lemon thyme
11½ oz. puff pastry
4 oz. Camembert, sliced
salt and pepper

one Lightly grease a baking sheet and sprinkle with water. Melt the butter in a frying pan, add the shallots, and gently sauté for 5 minutes until softened. Stir in the thyme.

two Roll out the pastry on a lightly floured surface to a 8 inch square and cut into 4 squares. Transfer to the prepared baking sheet. Using the tip of a sharp knife, make a shallow cut along each side of the squares, ½ inch from the edges, to form a rim.

three Spoon the shallots and thyme into the centers of the pastries. Bake in a preheated 425°F oven for 10 minutes until puffed. Arrange the cheese over the shallots and return to the oven for 5 minutes longer. Serve warm.

tofu, cinnamon, and honey pockets

2 tbsp. butter
2 onions, chopped
½ cup sliced almonds, lightly crushed
1 tbsp. honey
1 tsp. ground cinnamon
7 oz. tofu, drained and diced
5 oz. phyllo pastry
salt and pepper

one Melt half of the butter in a frying pan, add the onions and sauté for 3 minutes until softened. Stir in the almonds and sauté for 2 minutes until turning golden. Stir in the honey, cinnamon, and tofu, and season to taste with salt and pepper.

two Melt the remaining butter in a small saucepan. Cut out sixteen 7 inch squares from the phyllo pastry. Lay 8 squares on the surface and brush with a little melted butter. Cover each with a second square placed at an angle to create a star shape. Pile the tofu mixture on to the centers of the squares.

three Brush the edges of the pastry with a little butter. Bring the edges up over the filling and crimp together to make bundles. Repeat with the remaining pastries. Transfer to a baking sheet and brush with the remaining butter.

four Bake in a preheated 400°F oven for about 10 minutes or until the pastry is golden. Serve warm.

feta and tapenade drop scones

1¾ cup self-rising flour
1 tsp. baking powder
¼ tsp. salt
1 egg
1 cup milk
4 tbsp. Tapenade (see page 9)
7 oz. feta cheese, drained and diced
2 tsp. finely chopped rosemary
oil, for pan-frying
salt and pepper
mixed salad greens, to serve

These delicious little drop scone-style pancakes are perfect for a lunchtime or evening snack when you fancy something light but very savory. Excess batter and cheese mixture can be stored in the refrigerator for up to two days.

one Place the flour, baking powder, salt, and egg in a bowl. Gradually whisk in the milk to make a smooth batter. Alternatively, place all the ingredients in a food processor or blender and process until smooth.

two Mix together the tapenade, feta, and rosemary in a separate bowl. Heat a little oil in a large frying pan. Drop several separate tablespoonfuls of the batter into the pan so that they spread to about 3 inches in diameter. Cook gently until the batter is bubbling and just firm.

three Spoon a little of the cheese mixture on to the center of each, then carefully flip the pancakes with a spatula and pan-fry for another minute. Slide out of the pan and keep warm while cooking the remaining mixture in the same way. Serve the pancakes cheese side up with mixed salad greens.

lemon grass and tofu nuggets with chili sauce

1 bunch of scallions
2 in. piece of fresh ginger, peeled and chopped
2 lemon grass stalks, coarsely chopped
small handful of cilantro
3 garlic cloves, coarsely chopped
1 tbsp. sugar
1 tbsp. light soy sauce
10 oz. tofu, drained
½ cup breadcrumbs
1 egg
oil, for pan-frying
salt and pepper

Dipping sauce
1 tbsp. honey
2 tbsp. soy sauce
1 red chili, seeded and sliced
2 tbsp. orange juice

one Thinly slice 1 scallion and set aside. Coarsely chop the remainder and place in a food processor with the ginger, lemon grass, cilantro, and garlic and process lightly until mixed together and chopped but still chunky. Add the sugar, soy sauce, tofu, breadcrumbs, egg, and salt and pepper and process until just combined.

two Take teaspoonfuls of the mixture and pat into flat cakes using lightly floured hands.

three Mix together the ingredients for the dipping sauce, adding the reserved sliced scallion, in a small serving bowl.

four Heat the oil in a large, preferably nonstick, frying pan. Add half the tofu cakes and pan-fry gently for 1–2 minutes on each side until golden. Drain on paper towels and keep warm while frying the remainder. Serve with the dipping sauce.

Preparation time 15 minutes Cooking time 5 minutes Total time 20 minutes Serves 4

vegetable rice pancakes with sesame and ginger sauce

Sauce
1 garlic clove, coarsely chopped
3 tbsp. light brown sugar
2 in. piece fresh ginger, peeled and
coarsely chopped
4 tsp. soy sauce
5 tsp. wine or rice vinegar
2 tbsp. tomato purée
2 tbsp. sesame seeds, extra to garnish

Pancakes
8 rice pancakes, ready-made wonton or
spring roll wrappers
2 medium carrots
3½ oz. bean sprouts or mixed
sprouting beans
small handful of mint, coarsely chopped
1 celery stalk, thinly sliced
4 scallions, thinly sliced diagonally
1 tbsp. soy sauce

Paper-thin rice pancakes make interesting wraps for a feast of tempting fillings—here, a light vegetable version. Served with a highly flavored sauce, it makes an intriguing starter. Allow two rice pancakes per portion, but if there is a lot to follow, one is probably enough.

one Place all the ingredients for the sauce, except the sesame seeds, in a food processor (use the small bowl of a food processor if you have one) or blender and process to a thin paste. Alternatively, crush the garlic, grate the ginger, and whisk with the remaining ingredients. Stir in the sesame seeds and transfer to a serving bowl.

two Soften the rice pancakes according to the packet instructions. Cut the carrots into fine shreds and mix with the bean sprouts, mint, celery, scallions, and soy sauce.

three Divide the vegetable mixture between the 8 pancakes and spoon into the middle of each. Fold in the bottom edge of each pancake to the middle, then roll up from one side to the other to form a pocket.

four Steam the pancakes in a vegetable steamer or bamboo steamer for about 5 minutes until heated through. Alternatively, place on a wire rack set over a roasting pan of boiling water and cover with foil. Serve immediately with the sauce for spooning over, garnish with sesame seeds.

couscous, polenta, & grains

Couscous, polenta, bulgur, and millet take their place among a seemingly ever-expanding range of cereal-based products that are now widely available. They each add their own individual flavor and texture to vegetarian dishes, whether used as an integral ingredient or as a simple accompaniment.

couscous fritters with beets and sour cream

5 oz. couscous
7 tbsp. hot Vegetable Stock (see page 9)
4 scallions, finely chopped
2 garlic cloves, chopped
3 tbsp. chopped parsley
3 oz. pine nuts, coarsely chopped
2 oz. ground almonds
finely grated rind of 1 lemon
1 egg
oil, for frying
4 small cooked beets, cut into wedges
salt and pepper
flat leaf parsley, to garnish
sour cream, to serve

Dressing
4 tbsp. extra virgin olive oil
1 tsp. Tabasco sauce
1 tbsp. lemon juice

one Place two-thirds of the couscous in a bowl, add the vegetable stock, and let stand for 5 minutes. Meanwhile, mix together the ingredients for the dressing in a small bowl.

two When the couscous has absorbed all the stock, fluff up with a fork and stir in the scallions, garlic, parsley, pine nuts, almonds, lemon rind, and egg. Season with salt and pepper and mix until the ingredients bind together.

three Take heaped teaspoonfuls of the mixture and shape into balls. Roll them in the remaining couscous. Wet your hands before rolling the balls if the mixture starts to stick.

four Heat a 1 inch depth of oil in a sauté pan or heavy-bottomed saucepan. Add the couscous balls to the oil, half at a time, and sauté for about 2 minutes or until golden. Drain on paper towels while cooking the remainder.

five Arrange the beet wedges on serving plates and pile the fritters beside them. Top with a spoonful of crème fraîche, garnish with parsley, and serve with the dressing spooned over the top.

Preparation time 5 minutes Cooking time 25 minutes Total time 30 minutes Serves 4

spiced vegetable couscous

8 oz. couscous
4 tbsp. olive oil
1 large onion, chopped
3 garlic cloves, crushed
2 inch piece of fresh ginger, peeled and grated
½ tsp. dried chili flakes
2 tsp. each of paprika and ground cumin
1 tsp. ground turmeric
1 cinnamon stick, halved
1 medium sweet potato, scrubbed and diced
14 oz. can chickpeas, rinsed and drained
1½ cups Vegetable Stock (see page 9)
3 oz. raisins
salt and pepper
cilantro leaves, to garnish

one Place the couscous in a shallow ovenproof dish. Pour over 1 cup boiling water. Cover with a lid or foil and place in a preheated 300°F oven while preparing the vegetables.

two Heat the oil in a large saucepan or sauté pan. Add the onion, garlic, ginger, and spices and sauté, stirring gently, for 5 minutes until golden.

three Add the sweet potato, chickpeas, stock, and dried fruit. Season to taste with salt and pepper and bring to a boil. Reduce the heat, cover, and simmer for 20 minutes or until the potatoes are tender.

four Fluff up the couscous with a fork and spoon on to serving plates. Top with the vegetables and sauce, and serve scattered with cilantro leaves.

Preparation time 10 minutes Cooking time 20 minutes Total time 30 minutes Serves 4

soft polenta with gruyère and tomato sauce

8 oz. quick-cook polenta
3 garlic cloves, chopped
4 tbsp. olive oil
1 large onion, chopped
13 oz. can chopped tomatoes
3 tbsp. sun-dried tomato paste
2 tsp. light brown sugar
3 oz. Gruyère or cheddar cheese, grated
salt and pepper

A really quick and easy pantry supper dish that requires no more than a leafy green salad as an accompaniment. If you want to add extra flavor to the polenta, stir in some fresh chopped herbs, grated Parmesan, or a generous wad of butter.

one Bring 3½ cups water to a boil in a large saucepan with 1 tsp. salt. Add the polenta in a steady stream, then the garlic, and cook, stirring, for 5 minutes or until the polenta is very thick and pulpy. Turn into a lightly greased, shallow, ovenproof dish.

two Heat the oil in a saucepan. Add the onion and sauté for 5 minutes. Add the tomatoes, sun-dried tomato paste, and sugar to the onion and season to taste with salt and pepper. Spoon the mixture over the polenta.

three Scatter with the grated cheese and bake in a preheated 400°F oven for 10 minutes until golden.

green couscous with spiced fruit sauce

8 oz. couscous
2 cups plus 2 tbsp. hot Vegetable Stock (see page 9)
3 oz. unsalted, shelled pistachio nuts, coarsely chopped
2 scallions, chopped
small handful of parsley, chopped
14 oz. can flageolet or cannellini beans, rinsed and drained
½ tsp. saffron threads
1 tbsp. cardamom pods
2 tsp. coriander seeds
½ tsp. chili powder
4 tbsp. flaked almonds
3 oz. dried apricots
salt and pepper

To reveal their stunning emerald green color, pistachio nuts are best skinned by immersing them in boiling water for one minute, then rubbing off the skins between sheets of paper towels. Only do this if you have time since it is very time-consuming!

one Place the couscous in a bowl. Add 1 cup of the hot stock. Let stand for 5 minutes until the stock is absorbed, then stir in the pistachio nuts, scallions, parsley, and beans, season to taste with salt and pepper. Cover with a lid or foil and place in a preheated 300°F oven for 15 minutes.

two Meanwhile, place the saffron in a small cup with 1 tbsp. boiling water and leave for 3 minutes. Crush the cardamom pods using a mortar and pestle, or place the pods in a small bowl and crush with the end of a rolling pin. Pick out and discard the pods, then lightly crush the seeds.

three Transfer to a food processor or blender with the coriander seeds, chili powder, almonds, and apricots. Process until finely chopped. Add the saffron and soaking liquid, the remaining stock, and salt and pepper and blend until pulpy. Transfer to a saucepan and heat through for 1 minute. Serve with the couscous.

tabbouleh with fruit and nuts

5 oz. bulgur
³/₄ cup unsalted, shelled pistachio nuts
1 small red onion, finely chopped
3 garlic cloves, crushed
1 oz. flat leaf parsley, chopped
½ oz. mint, chopped
finely grated rind and juice of 1 lemon or lime
1 cup pitted prunes, sliced
4 tbsp. olive oil
salt and pepper

An abundance of herbs gives this salad its wonderful flavor. If prunes are not your favorite dried fruit, substitute just about any other—apricots or raisins. Figs and dates are also good in this recipe.

one Place the bulgur in a bowl, cover with plenty of boiling water, and leave for 15 minutes.

two Meanwhile, place the pistachio nuts in a separate bowl and cover with boiling water. Let stand for 1 minute, then drain. Rub the nuts between several thicknesses of paper towels to remove most of the skins, then peel away any remaining skins with the fingers.

three Mix the nuts with the onion, garlic, parsley, mint, lemon or lime rind and juice, and prunes in a large bowl.

four Drain the bulgur thoroughly in a sieve, pressing out as much moisture as possible with the back of a spoon. Add to the other ingredients with the oil and toss together. Chill until ready to serve.

mushroom, couscous, and herb sausages

3 oz. couscous
3 tbsp. olive oil
1 onion, chopped
8 oz. chestnut mushrooms, coarsely chopped
1 red chili, seeded and finely sliced
3 garlic cloves, coarsely chopped
small handful of mixed herbs, such as thyme, rosemary, parsley
7 oz. whole cooked chestnuts
3 oz. breadcrumbs
1 egg yolk
oil, for pan-frying
salt and pepper

A richly flavored, wintry main course. Serve simply with cranberry relish or plenty of golden fried onions, gravy, and buttery mashed potatoes. precooked chestnuts are usually available in vacuum packs, the perfect convenience food.

one Place the couscous in a bowl, 6 tbsp. boiling water and let stand for 5 minutes.

two Meanwhile, heat the olive oil in a frying pan, add the onion, mushrooms, and chili and sauté quickly for about 5 minutes or until the mushrooms are golden and the moisture has evaporated.

three Transfer to a food processor or blender with the garlic, herbs, and chestnuts and process until finely chopped. Turn into a bowl and add the soaked couscous, breadcrumbs, egg yolk, and salt and pepper.

four Using lightly floured hands, shape the mixture into 12 sausage shapes. Heat the oil for pan-frying and fry the sausages for about 5 minutes, turning frequently.

Preparation time 10 minutes   Cooking time 20 minutes   Total time 30 minutes   Serves 4

polenta fries with saffron mushrooms

1 tsp. saffron threads
1 lb. ready-cooked polenta
1 tbsp. all-purpose flour
2 tsp. chili powder
oil, for pan-frying
1 tbsp. butter
1 onion, chopped
2 garlic cloves, crushed
13 oz. mixed wild and cultivated mushrooms, halved if large
8 oz. mascarpone cheese
2 tbsp. chopped tarragon
finely grated rind and juice of ½ lemon
salt and pepper

Unless you have the time to cook and set homemade polenta, use a pack of ready-cooked polenta to make these chips. Tossed in chili powder and pan-fried, they make a welcome change to the more traditional potato chips.

one Place the saffron in a bowl with 1 tbsp. boiling water and let stand until needed.

two Cut the polenta into ½ inch slices, then cut the slices into ½ inch strips. Mix together the flour, chili powder, and salt and pepper and use to coat the polenta.

three Heat a ½ inch depth of oil in a frying pan and fry the polenta, half at a time, for about 10 minutes or until golden. Once cooked, drain on paper towels and keep warm.

four While the polenta is cooking, melt the butter in a separate frying pan or sauté pan, add the onion and garlic and sauté for 5 minutes. Stir in the mushrooms and sauté for 2 minutes. Add the mascarpone, tarragon, lemon rind and juice, saffron, and soaking liquid, and season to taste with salt and pepper. Stir until the mascarpone has melted to make a sauce. Serve with the polenta fries.

Preparation time 5 minutes   Cooking time 25 minutes   Total time 30 minutes   Serves 4

spiced millet

2 tbsp. butter
1 onion, chopped
2 garlic cloves, crushed
1 tbsp. cardamom pods, lightly crushed
2 tsp. whole cloves
1 cinnamon stick, halved
7 oz. millet
2 cups Vegetable Stock (see page 9)
4 tbsp. chopped parsley
salt and pepper

Millet is a small, golden grain that looks a little like couscous. Its mild flavor and light texture are best dressed up with spices, making it a perfect alternative to rice as an accompaniment to spicy stews and bean dishes. Add some drained, canned lentils and a spoonful of harissa paste to turn this dish into a main course.

one Melt the butter in a heavy-bottomed saucepan. Add the onion and sauté gently for 3 minutes. Add the garlic, cardamom pods, cloves, cinnamon, and millet. Season to taste with salt and pepper and sauté for 2 minutes.

two Add the stock and bring to a boil. Reduce the heat and simmer gently, uncovered, for about 20 minutes or until the millet is tender and the stock absorbed. Lightly fluff up the millet a couple of times during cooking to keep the grains light and separate. Serve hot.

salads &
side salads

Creativity is the key when it comes to salads, composing with several carefully selected complementary ingredients to create a feast of color, flavor, and texture. Some of the salads presented are sufficiently sustaining to serve as main courses, while others make attractive starters or imaginative side dishes.

sweet potato, arugula, and haloumi salad

1 lb. sweet potatoes, sliced
3 tbsp. olive oil
8 oz. haloumi cheese, patted dry on kitchen paper
3 oz. arugula

Dressing
5 tbsp. olive oil
3 tbsp. honey
2 tbsp. lemon or lime juice
1½ tsp. black onion seeds
1 red chili, seeded and finely sliced
2 tsp. chopped lemon thyme
salt and pepper

This combination of firm, salty cheese, sweet potato, and a honeyed, spiced, citrus dressing is absolutely delicious. This quantity serves 4 as a light lunch or supper dish, or 6 as a starter.

one Mix together all the ingredients for the dressing in a small bowl.

two Cook the sweet potatoes in lightly salted, boiling water for 2 minutes. Drain well. Heat the oil in a large frying pan, add the sweet potatoes, and sauté for about 10 minutes, turning once, until golden.

three Meanwhile, thinly slice the cheese and place on a lightly oiled foil-lined grill rack. Cook under a preheated moderate grill for about 3 minutes until golden.

four Pile the sweet potatoes, cheese and arugula on to serving plates and spoon over the dressing.

ribboned carrot salad

4 medium carrots
2 celery stalks
1 bunch of scallions
4 tbsp. light olive oil
2 tbsp. lime juice
2 tsp. sugar
¼ teaspoon crushed dried chilies
2 tbsp. chopped mint
½ cup salted peanuts
salt and pepper

This is the lightest, prettiest, salad imaginable, perfect for accompanying a main course such as pasta or pizza. Use a mandoline or potato peeler to pare the carrots and leave the vegetables in the iced water until shortly before serving as they gradually uncurl after draining.

one Half fill a medium bowl with very cold water, adding a few ice cubes if necessary.

two Peel the carrots and pare off as many long ribbons as you can from each. Place the ribbons in the water. Cut the celery into 2 inch lengths. Cut each length into very thin slices. Cut the scallions into 2 inch lengths and shred lengthwise. Add the celery and scallions to the water and leave for 15–20 minutes until the vegetables curl up.

three Mix together the oil, lime juice, sugar, chilies, and mint in a small bowl and season to taste with salt and pepper.

four Thoroughly drain the vegetables and toss in a salad bowl with the dressing, peanuts, and salt and pepper. Serve immediately.

Preparation time 10 minutes Cooking time 10 minutes Total time 20 minutes Serves 4

grilled baby eggplant and tomato salad

9 oz. baby eggplants
4 tbsp. olive oil
1 tbsp. lemon juice
2 tbsp. coarsely chopped chervil or parsley
8 oz. cherry tomatoes, halved
1 teaspoon sugar
2 garlic cloves, crushed
7 oz. ricotta cheese
2 oz. arugula
4 tsp. balsamic vinegar
salt and pepper

Serve this colorful salad either as a starter for 4 or a more substantial supper for 2. Although very appealing, baby eggplants are not widely available, so substitute a large eggplant, thickly sliced, if you cannot find any.

one Halve the eggplants and cut criss-cross lines over the cut surfaces for decoration. Place, cut sides up, on a foil-lined broiler pan and drizzle with 1 tbsp. of the oil, the lemon juice, and salt and pepper. Broil under a preheated hot broiler for 8–10 minutes, turning once, until tender and golden, then sprinkle with the chervil or parsley.

two Meanwhile, place the tomatoes in a frying pan with another tbsp. of the oil and sprinkle with the sugar, garlic, and salt and pepper. Sauté quickly for 1–2 minutes until softened but not mushy.

three Arrange the eggplants on warmed serving plates, pile the ricotta, then the tomatoes, and finally the arugula on top. Add the balsamic vinegar, remaining oil, salt and pepper, and any juices on the foil to the frying pan and heat through for 30 seconds. Pour over the salad to serve.

thai-dressed tofu rolls

1 small iceburg lettuce
9 oz. tofu, diced
3½ oz. snow peas, shredded lengthwise
2 tbsp. sesame oil
2 tbsp. light soy sauce
2 tbsp. lime juice
1 tbsp. brown sugar
1 Thai chili, seeded and sliced
1 garlic clove, crushed
pepper

one Remove 8 leaves from the lettuce. Fill a large heatproof bowl with boiling water. Add the separated leaves and leave for 10 seconds. Rinse in cold water and drain thoroughly.

two Finely shred the remaining lettuce and toss in a bowl with the tofu and snow peas.

three Mix together the sesame oil, soy sauce, lime juice, sugar, chili, garlic, and pepper and add to the tofu. Toss together gently.

four Spoon a little mixture on to the center of each blanched lettuce leaf, then roll up. Chill until ready to serve.

beet salad with cilantro and tomato salsa

8 medium cooked beets, sliced
2 tbsp. red wine vinegar
1 teaspoon sugar
2 tbsp. light olive oil
salt and pepper
crème fraîche, to serve
cilantro sprigs, to garnish

Salsa
1 red onion, finely chopped
14 oz. small vine-ripened tomatoes, seeded and chopped
2 garlic cloves, crushed
½ oz. cilantro, chopped

one Toss the beets in a bowl with the vinegar, sugar, oil, and salt and pepper.

two Mix together the ingredients for the salsa in a separate bowl. Season lightly with salt and pepper.

three Arrange about two-thirds of the beet slices on 4 serving plates. Pile the salsa on to the beets, then add the remaining beet slices. Top with spoonfuls of crème fraîche and spoon over any dressing left in the beet bowl. Serve garnished with cilantro sprigs.

spiced orange and avocado salad

4 large juicy oranges
2 small ripe avocados, pitted and peeled
2 tsp. cardamom pods
3 tbsp. light olive oil
1 tbsp. honey
good pinch of ground allspice
2 tsp. lemon juice
salt and pepper
watercress sprigs, to garnish

one Peel the oranges, then cut away the white skin. Working over a bowl to catch the juices, cut between the membranes to remove the segments.

two Slice the avocados and toss gently with the orange segments. Pile on to serving plates.

three Reserve a few whole cardamom pods for decoration. Crush the remaining pods using a mortar and pestle to extract the seeds, or place in a small bowl and crush with the end of a rolling pin. Pick out and discard the pods. Mix the seeds with the oil, honey, allspice, lemon juice, salt and pepper, and reserved orange juice.

four Garnish the salads with the watercress sprigs and serve with the dressing spooned over the top.

herb salad with stem ginger and grapes

1 small head of fennel, finely chopped
8 oz. seedless green grapes, halved
2 pieces of bottled stem ginger, finely chopped, plus
2 tbsp. syrup from the jar
4 tbsp. grape or apple juice
2 tbsp. olive oil
5 oz. mixed herbs or salad greens
½ cup unsalted cashews or walnuts (optional)
salt and pepper

This refreshing, summery side salad can easily be transformed into a main course with the addition of diced smoked tofu or goat cheese. Serve with a whole-grain bread.

one In a medium bowl, mix together the fennel, grapes, ginger and ginger syrup, fruit juice, and oil, and season to taste with salt and pepper.

two Place the salad leaves in a serving bowl and add the nuts, if using. Add the other ingredients and toss together lightly before serving.

panzanella

3 red bell peppers, cored, seeded, and quartered
12 oz. ripe plum tomatoes, skinned
6 tbsp. extra virgin olive oil
3 tbsp. wine vinegar
2 garlic cloves, crushed
1 cup stale italian bread
½ cup pitted black olives
small handful of basil leaves, shredded
salt and pepper

In this classic Italian salad, pieces of italian bread are tossed with the other ingredients, absorbing the wonderful flavor of the garlicky tomato dressing. It is best to use slightly stale Italian bread which will not fall apart. Alternatively, use lightly toasted fresh bread. This quantity serves 4 as a starter or 2 as a main course.

one Place the peppers, skin side up, on a foil-lined broiler pan and broil under a preheated moderate broiler for 10 minutes or until the skins are blackened.

two Meanwhile, quarter the tomatoes and scoop out the pulp, placing it in a sieve over a bowl to catch the juices. Set the tomato quarters aside. Press the pulp with the back of a spoon to extract as much juice as possible.

three Beat the oil, vinegar, garlic, and salt and pepper into the tomato juice.

four When cool enough to handle, peel the skins from the peppers and discard. Coarsely slice the peppers and place in a bowl with the tomato quarters. Break the bread into small chunks and add to the bowl with the olives and basil.

five Add the dressing and toss the ingredients together before serving.

potato and green bean salad

1¾ lb. new potatoes, scrubbed
5 oz. green beans, halved
6 tbsp. extra virgin olive oil
4 tsp. lemon juice
2 tsp. pink peppercorns
1 teaspoon sugar
4 tbsp. chopped chives
4 eggs
salt and pepper
watercress or sorrel, to serve

This lovely Niçoise-style salad is great to make when interesting salad potatoes are available, such as the red- or purple-skinned varieties. Serve as a light snack or starter, in which case some dainty quail eggs could be substituted for the ordinary eggs. Boil them for two minutes only.

one Cook the potatoes in plenty of lightly salted boiling water for about 15 minutes or until just tender.

two Meanwhile, cook the green beans in a separate pan of boiling water for 2–3 minutes or until just tender. Drain and refresh under cold water.

three Mix together the oil, lemon juice, peppercorns, sugar, chives, and salt and pepper in a bowl.

four Lower the eggs into a small saucepan of boiling water and cook for 4 minutes. (Cook the eggs for an extra 3 minutes if you prefer them hard-boiled.) Drain.

five Drain the potatoes, then plunge in a bowl of water to cool. Drain. Shell and quarter the eggs.

six Toss the potatoes, green beans, and eggs in the dressing. Pile on to a bed of watercress or sorrel on individual serving plates.

vegetable dishes

Vegetarian cooking thrives on the amazing array of exotic, seasonal, and everyday vegetables that we can now readily buy, and the many different ways in which they can be cooked. Here, fresh herbs, fragrant spices, and other subtle seasonings are used to bring out the essential flavors of the ingredients to create delicious main meals, snacks, and accompaniments.

Preparation time 10 minutes Cooking time 10 minutes Total time 20 minutes Serves 4

celeriac and potato remoulade with asparagus

1 lb. celeriac, peeled
12 oz. potatoes, peeled
1 tbsp. extra virgin olive oil, plus extra for drizzling (optional)
1 lb. asparagus, trimmed

Sauce
½ cup mayonnaise
½ cup yogurt
1 tsp. Dijon mustard
6 cocktail gherkins, finely chopped
2 tbsp. capers, chopped
2 tbsp. chopped tarragon
salt and pepper

To make this summery lunch or supper dish more substantial, lightly poach some eggs in a little vinegared water and arrange them over the asparagus.

one Cut the celeriac and potato into matchstick-sized pieces, but keep the two vegetables separate. Cook the celeriac in lightly salted boiling water for 2 minutes or until softened. Add the potatoes and cook for a further 2 minutes or until just tender. Drain the vegetables and refresh under running water.

two Meanwhile, mix together the ingredients for the sauce and set aside.

three Heat the oil in a frying pan or griddle pan. Add the asparagus and sauté for 2–3 minutes or until just beginning to color.

four Mix the celeriac and potato with the sauce and spoon on to 4 serving plates. Top with the asparagus spears.

five Serve immediately, drizzled with a little extra olive oil, if desired.

Preparation time 5 minutes Cooking time 7 minutes Total time 12 minutes Serves 2

deviled mushrooms on brioche

4 tsp. mango chutney
¾ inch piece of fresh ginger, grated
2 tbsp. Worcestershire sauce
1 tbsp. coarse grain mustard
2 tsp. paprika
5 tbsp. fresh orange juice
2 brioche buns or 2 large slices of brioche
1 tbsp. butter
1 tbsp. oil
3 shallots, thinly sliced
8 oz. chestnut mushrooms, halved
2 tbsp. sour cream

one Cut up any large pieces of mango and mix the chutney with the ginger, Worcestershire sauce, mustard, paprika, and orange juice.

two Thickly slice the buns, if using, and toast the brioche. Keep warm.

three Melt the butter in a frying pan with the oil. Add the shallots and sauté gently for 3 minutes or until softened. Add the mushrooms and sauté quickly for about 3 minutes, stirring, until golden.

four Add the chutney mixture to the pan and heat through for 1 minute, then stir in the cream. Spoon over the toasted brioche and serve hot.

Preparation time 5 minutes Cooking time 2 minutes Total time 7 minutes Serves 4

wilted spinach with pine nuts and raisins

½ cup plump raisins
3 tbsp. olive oil
½ cup pine nuts
2 garlic cloves, crushed
1¼ lb. baby spinach
finely grated rind of 1 lemon
salt and pepper

This refreshing combination of flavors makes a good accompaniment to pizza, bean, or pasta dishes, or serve as a light tapas on its own to excite the appetite.

one Place the raisins in a small bowl, cover with boiling water and leave for 5 minutes.

two Meanwhile, heat the oil in a large frying pan or sauté pan and sauté the pine nuts until pale golden. Stir in the garlic.

three Thoroughly drain the raisins and add to the pan with the spinach. Cook for about 1 minute, turning the ingredients together until the spinach has just wilted. Add the lemon rind, season to taste with salt and pepper, and serve immediately.

Preparation time 10 minutes Cooking time 10 minutes Total time 20 minutes Serves 4

deep-fried zucchini with minted yogurt

3 medium zucchini
1 small onion, very thinly sliced
1 egg
½ tsp medium curry paste
7 tbsp. all-purpose flour
oil, for deep-frying
salt and pepper

Minted yogurt
3½ oz. yogurt
2 tbsp. chopped mint

In this simple starter, grated zucchini are coated in a light-as-air tempura-style batter to make crisp, golden, little vegetable bundles. The batter and vegetables can be prepared ahead, but do not mix them together until you are ready for frying.

one Coarsely grate the zucchini and mix in a bowl with the onion.

two In a separate bowl, beat the egg with the curry paste and 7 tbsp. cold water. Whisk in the flour. Add the zucchini and onions and mix until evenly combined.

three Mix the yogurt with the mint in a small serving dish.

four Heat a 2 inch depth of oil in a deep-fat fryer or large, heavy-bottomed saucepan until a drop of the batter sizzles and rises to the surface. Add heaping teaspoonfuls of the batter to the pan and fry for about 3 minutes until crisp and golden. Drain on paper towels and keep warm while cooking the remainder. You will probably need to fry the batter in 3 batches. Serve with the minted yogurt.

mushroom toad-in-the-hole with beer and onion gravy

4 large Portabella mushrooms, or
13 oz. smaller mushrooms
1 tbsp. butter
5 tbsp. olive oil
3 garlic cloves, sliced
2 tbsp. chopped rosemary or thyme
1 cup all-purpose flour
2 eggs
2 tbsp. hot horseradish sauce
1¾ cup milk
2 onions, sliced
2 tsp. sugar
1 cup and 2 tbsp. stout
½ cup Vegetable Stock (see page 9)
salt and pepper

one Place the mushrooms, stem side up, in a large shallow ovenproof dish. Melt the butter with 4 tbsp. of the oil in a frying pan. Add the garlic and herbs, season to taste with salt and pepper, and stir for 30 seconds. Pour over the mushrooms and bake in a preheated 450°F oven for 2 minutes.

two Meanwhile, blend the flour, eggs, horseradish, milk, and a little salt in a food processor or blender until smooth. Alternatively, place the flour in a bowl and gradually whisk in the eggs, horseradish, milk, and salt and pepper.

three Pour the batter over the mushrooms and bake for 20–25 minutes until or until the batter is puffed and golden.

four Meanwhile, heat the remaining oil in a frying pan. Add the onions and sugar and sauté for about 5 minutes until deep golden. Add the beer and stock and salt and pepper. Cook, stirring frequently, for 5 minutes. Serve poured over the mushroom batter.

spaghetti squash with cabbage and nuts

1 spaghetti squash, weighing about 3 lb
1½ tbsp. butter
1 onion, thinly sliced
2 garlic cloves, crushed
5 oz. green cabbage, finely shredded
½ cup natural peanuts or cashews
3½ oz. crème fraîche
plenty of freshly grated nutmeg
salt and pepper

Spaghetti squash is a remarkable vegetable in the way that the flesh can be shredded, once cooked, into thousands of spaghetti-like threads. Serve it tossed in butter or olive oil as an accompaniment, or turn it into a quick and easy main course with cabbage and nuts.

one Place the squash in a large pan in which it just fits. Cover with boiling water and boil for 20 minutes.

two Meanwhile, melt the butter in a frying pan and gently sauté the onion and garlic for 5 minutes. Stir in the cabbage and sauté for 3 minutes until tender. Add the nuts, crème fraîche, and nutmeg, season to taste with salt and pepper, and cook until the crème fraîche melts to make a sauce.

three Drain and halve the spaghetti squash, and discard the seeds from the center. Using 2 forks, shred the flesh into a bowl, breaking it up into fine threads. Add to the frying pan and toss the ingredients together over the heat for 1 minute. Serve immediately.

baby squash with red bean sauce

2 cups Vegetable Stock (see page 9)
2 lb. mixed baby squash, such as gem, butternut, or acorn
4 oz. baby spinach

Sauce
4 tbsp. olive oil
4 garlic cloves, thinly sliced
1 red bell pepper, cored, seeded, and finely chopped
2 tomatoes, chopped
14 oz. can red kidney beans, rinsed and drained
1–2 tbsp. hot chili sauce
small handful of chopped cilantro
salt

To serve
steamed white rice
sour cream (optional)
avocado and lime salad (optional)

This is a great dish to make during the autumn, when various baby squash and pumpkin are at their most plentiful.

one Bring the stock to a boil in a large saucepan. Quarter and seed the squash or pumpkin. Add to the pan, reduce the heat, and cover. Simmer gently for about 15 minutes or until just tender.

two Meanwhile, to make the sauce, heat the oil in a frying pan, add the garlic and pepper and sauté for 5 minutes, stirring frequently, until very soft. Add the tomatoes, red kidney beans, chili sauce, and a little salt and simmer for 5 minutes until pulpy.

three Drain the squash or pumpkin from the stock, reserving the stock, and return to the pan. Scatter over the spinach leaves, cover and cook for about 1 minute until the spinach has wilted.

four Pile the vegetables on to steamed rice on serving plates. Stir 8 tbsp. of the reserved stock into the sauce with the cilantro. Spoon over the vegetables and serve with sour cream and an avocado and lime salad if desired.

Preparation time 5 minutes   Cooking time 15 minutes   Total time 20 minutes   Serves 3–4

watercress and mushroom frittata

6 eggs
5 tbsp. grated Parmesan cheese
1 bunch of watercress, tough stems removed
1½ tbsp. butter
8 oz. mushrooms, thinly sliced
salt and pepper

A frittata is an Italian-style omelette and, like an omelette, can be flavored in many interesting ways. For best results, use a good-quality, heavy-bottomed frying pan and really fresh, flavorful eggs.

one Beat the eggs in a bowl with a fork to break them up. Stir in the Parmesan, watercress, and plenty of salt and pepper.

two Melt the butter in a heavy-bottomed frying pan. Add the mushrooms and sauté quickly for 3 minutes. Pour in the egg mixture and gently stir the ingredients together.

three Reduce the heat to its lowest setting and sauté gently until the mixture is lightly set and the underside is golden when the edge of the frittata is lifted with a spatula. If the base of the omelette starts to brown before the top is set, place it under a moderate grill to finish cooking.

Preparation time 10 minutes   Cooking time 15 minutes   Total time 25 minutes   Serves 4

basil and tomato stew

2 lb. ripe tomatoes, skinned
6 tbsp. olive oil
2 onions, chopped
4 celery stalks, sliced
4 plump garlic cloves, thinly sliced
6 oz. mushrooms, sliced
3 tbsp. sun-dried tomato paste
2 cups Vegetable Stock (see page 9)
1 tbsp. brown sugar
3 tbsp. capers
large handful of basil leaves, about ½ oz
large handful of chervil or flat leaf parsley, about ½ oz
salt and pepper
warm bread, to serve

Save making this stew for when you can find really juicy, flavorful tomatoes. Most ordinary supermarket varieties will give a thin, watery result.

one Quarter and seed the tomatoes, scooping out the pulp into a sieve over a bowl to catch the juices.

two Heat 4 tbsp. of the oil in a large saucepan and sauté the onions and celery for 5 minutes. Add the garlic and mushrooms and sauté for 3 minutes longer.

three Add the tomatoes and their juices, sun-dried tomatoes, stock, sugar, and capers and bring to a boil. Reduce the heat and simmer gently, uncovered, for 5 minutes.

four Tear the herbs into pieces, add to the pan with a little salt and pepper, and cook for 1 minute. Ladle into bowls, drizzle with the remaining oil, and serve with warm bread.

Preparation time 5 minutes Cooking time 20 minutes Total time 25 minutes Serves 4

baked vine tomatoes
with garlic and herbs

1 lb. vine-ripened tomatoes
2 plump garlic cloves, thinly sliced
1 tbsp. coarsely chopped thyme or rosemary
2 red chilies, halved lengthwise
5 tbsp. extra virgin olive oil
4 tbsp. balsamic vinegar
salt and pepper

one Cut the tomatoes from the vine in clumps of 2 or 3. Make a deep slit in each tomato and insert a couple of garlic slices, a good pinch of herbs, and season to taste with salt and pepper. Pack into a shallow ovenproof dish.

two Tuck the chili halves around the tomatoes. Pour over the oil and vinegar, season to taste with salt and pepper, then bake in a preheated 425°F oven for 20 minutes until the tomatoes are softened but not falling apart.

eggplant pâté

1 oz. dried porcini mushrooms
1 lb. eggplant
6 tbsp. olive oil
1 small red onion, chopped
2 tsp. cumin seeds
6 oz. button or chestnut mushrooms
2 garlic cloves, crushed
3 pickled walnuts, halved
small handful of cilantro
salt and pepper
toasted walnut or whole-grain bread, to serve

Just a few dried mushrooms really boost the flavor of this quick and easy pâté. It makes plenty and leftovers keep well in the refrigerator for several days, ready for either zipping up vegetable stews or spreading on to toast and grilling with Gruyère cheese.

one Place the dried mushrooms in a bowl and cover with plenty of boiling water. Leave to soak for 10 minutes.

two Meanwhile, cut the eggplant into ½ inch dice. Heat the oil in a large frying pan. Add the eggplant and onion and sauté gently for 8 minutes until the vegetables are softened and browned.

three Drain the dried mushrooms and add to the pan with the cumin seeds, fresh mushrooms, and garlic. Sauté for 5–7 minutes more until the eggplant are very soft.

four Transfer to a food processor or blender with the pickled walnuts and cilantro, season to taste with salt and pepper and process until broken up but not completely smooth. Transfer to a serving dish and serve warm or cold with toast.

Preparation time 10 minutes Cooking time 5 minutes Total time 15 minutes Serves 4-6

vegetable chips

8 oz. each potato, parsnip, and raw beets
oil, for deep-frying
coarse sea salt and pepper

Although not substantial enough to serve as a vegetable dish, these vegetable chips are fun to make and are a good accompaniment to drinks, rather like the trendy store-bought vegetable chips.

one Cut the vegetables into very thin slices using the slicer attachment of a food processor, or a mandoline. They can also be sliced by hand, although it can be difficult to get them sufficiently fine. Pat the vegetables dry on paper towels.

two Pour the oil into a deep-fat fryer or heavy-bottomed saucepan until about a third full. Heat the oil until a piece of vegetable sizzles on the surface. Add a batch of vegetable slices to the oil and fry until crisp and golden. Drain on paper towels while frying the remainder. Serve generously seasoned with salt and pepper.

Preparation time 8 minutes Cooking time 12 minutes Total time 20 minutes Serves 4

buttered cauliflower crumble

1 large cauliflower
1 tbsp. butter
½ cup breadcrumbs
2 tbsp. olive oil
3 tbsp. capers
3 cocktail gherkins, finely chopped
3 tbsp. chopped dill or tarragon
3½ oz. crème fraîche
4 tbsp. grated Parmesan cheese
salt and pepper

Sautéing cauliflower in butter brings out its flavor far more than the traditional boiling or steaming. The resulting dish is good enough to serve as a light meal on its own or as an accompaniment to bean or rice dishes.

one Cut the cauliflower into large florets and blanch in boiling water for 2 minutes. Drain thoroughly.

two Melt half of the butter in a large frying pan. Add the breadcrumbs and sauté for 2 minutes or until golden. Drain and set aside.

three Melt the remaining butter in the pan with the oil. Add the cauliflower florets and sauté gently for about 5 minutes or until golden. Add the capers, gherkins, dill or tarragon, and crème fraîche, season to taste with salt and pepper and stir over moderate heat for 1 minute.

four Turn into a shallow flameproof dish and sprinkle with the fried breadcrumbs and Parmesan. Cook under a preheated moderate broiler for about 2 minutes or until the crumbs are dark golden brown.

pan-fried roots with cardamom and honey

9 oz. small turnips, cut into wedges
1 small sweet potato, scrubbed and cut into chunks
9 oz. medium parsnips, cut into wedges
8 shallots, peeled but left whole
1 tbsp. cardamom pods
2 tbsp. honey
2 tsp. lemon juice
4 tbsp. olive oil
salt and pepper

Crushed cardamom seeds are delicious with root vegetables, bringing out their sweet, earthy flavors. Serve as an accompaniment to vegetable pancakes and spicy rice and bean dishes.

one Cook the turnips, sweet potato, parsnips and shallots in lightly salted boiling water for 7–8 minutes until softened but not tender.

two Meanwhile, crush the cardamom pods using a mortar and pestle to release the seeds. Alternatively, crush the pods in a small bowl using the end of a rolling pin. Pick out and discard the pods, then pound the seeds to crush them slightly. Mix with the honey, lemon juice, and a little salt and pepper.

three Drain the vegetables. Heat the oil in a large frying pan. Add the vegetables and sauté for about 6 minutes or until golden, stirring frequently. Add the cardamom dressing and toss together for 1 minute. Serve hot.

desserts & baked goods

Simple cooking techniques such as pan-frying, baking, and broiling capitalize on the many winning qualities of fresh, ripe fruits to create irresistible desserts with the minimum of time and fuss. Baked goods, too, can be quick as well as rewarding to make, providing a ready supply of luxurious snacks, and indulgent sweet treats.

Preparation time 10 minutes Cooking time 12 minutes Total time 22 minutes Makes 10

cranberry, oatmeal, and cinnamon scones

1½ cups self-rising flour
1 tsp. baking powder
1 tsp. ground cinnamon
3 tbsp. unsalted butter
¼ cup plus two tbsp. sugar
½ cup oatmeal, plus extra for sprinkling
¾ cup dried cranberries
5–6 tbsp. milk
beaten egg or milk, to glaze

Like all scones, these sweet fruit-specked ones are best served freshly baked, or frozen ahead and then warmed through to serve.

one Grease a baking sheet. Place the flour, baking powder, and cinnamon in a food processor. Add the butter, cut into small pieces, and process until the mixture resembles breadcrumbs. Add the sugar and oatmeal and blend briefly. Alternatively, rub the butter into the flour, baking powder, and cinnamon in a bowl, then add the sugar and oatmeal.

two Add the cranberries and milk and blend briefly until the mixture forms a soft dough, adding a little more milk if necessary.

three Turn out on to a floured surface and roll out to ¾ inch thick. Cut out rounds using a 2 inch cutter. Transfer to the prepared baking sheet and re-roll the trimmings to make more scones.

four Brush with beaten egg or milk and sprinkle with oatmeal. Bake in a preheated 425°F oven for 10–12 minutes until risen and golden. Transfer to a wire rack to cool. Serve split and buttered.

Preparation time 10 minutes Cooking time 15 minutes Total time 25 minutes Serves 6

plum and amaretto tartlets

12 oz. puff pastry
a little beaten egg, to glaze
6 oz. white or golden almond paste
powdered sugar, for dusting
1 lb. red or yellow plums, halved and pitted
4 tbsp. Amaretto liqueur or brandy
lightly whipped cream, to serve

This unbelievably easy dessert is perfect for any occasion, whether you are entertaining friends or in desperate need of something sweet and delicious.

one Lightly grease a baking sheet and sprinkle with water. Roll out the pastry on a lightly floured surface and cut out six 4 inch rounds using a cutter or small saucer as a guide. Using the tip of a sharp knife, make a shallow cut ½ inch from the edge of each round to form a rim. Brush the tops with beaten egg and transfer to the baking sheet.

two Roll out the almond paste on a surface dusted with powdered sugar and cut out six 3 inch rounds. Place a round in the center of each tartlet. Arrange the plum halves over the almond paste, cut sides up, and drizzle with as much liqueur or brandy as the cavities will hold. Bake in a preheated 425°F oven for about 15 minutes until the pastry is puffed.

three Spoon over any remaining liqueur and dust with powdered sugar. Serve with whipped cream.

chunky oat cookies

4 tbsp. unsalted butter, softened
½ cup plus 2 tbsp. golden brown sugar
1 egg
2 tsp. vanilla extract
1 cup rolled oats
4 tbsp. sunflower seeds
1¼ cups all-purpose flour
½ tsp. baking powder
6 oz. white chocolate, chopped into small pieces
icing sugar, for dusting

Use good-quality white chocolate without the oversweet, cloying taste of cheaper chocolate, or use milk or dark if preferred.

one Lightly grease a large baking sheet. Beat together the butter and sugar in a bowl until creamy. Add the egg, vanilla, oats, sunflower seeds, flour, and baking powder and mix to make a thick paste. Stir in the chocolate.

two Place teaspoonfuls of the mixture on the prepared baking sheet and flatten slightly with the back of a fork.

three Bake in a preheated 350°F oven for about 15 minutes or until puffed and golden. Leave for 5 minutes, then transfer to a wire rack to cool. Serve dusted with powdered sugar.

quick tiramisu

5 tbsp. strong espresso coffee
6 tbsp. dark brown sugar
4 tbsp. coffee liqueur or 3 tbsp. brandy
3 oz. lady fingers, broken into large pieces
13 oz. good-quality ready-made custard
8 oz. mascarpone cheese
1 tsp. vanilla extract
2 oz. plain chocolate, finely chopped
cocoa powder, for dusting

one Mix the coffee with 2 tbsp. of the sugar and the liqueur or brandy in a medium bowl. Toss the lady fingers in the mixture and turn into a serving dish, spooning over any excess liquid.

two Beat together the custard, mascarpone, and vanilla and spoon a third over the biscuits. Sprinkle with the remaining sugar, then half the remaining custard. Scatter with the chopped chocolate, then spread with the remaining custard.

three Chill for about 1 hour or until set. Serve dusted with cocoa powder.

pan-fried apricots with gingered mascarpone

2 pieces of bottled stem ginger, plus
2 tbsp. syrup from the jar
8 oz. mascarpone
2 tsp. lemon juice
2 tbsp. unsalted butter
2 tbsp. light brown sugar
13 oz. fresh apricots, halved
3 tbsp. Amaretto liqueur or brandy

A simple dessert that makes the most of fresh apricots during their all-too-short season. When not available, it is equally good made with red or yellow plums. Amaretti or ratafia biscuits make a no-fuss accompaniment.

one Finely chop the ginger and mix with the mascarpone, lemon juice, and ginger syrup.

two Melt the butter in a frying pan and add the sugar. Cook for about 1 minute until the sugar has dissolved. Add the apricots and sauté quickly until lightly colored but still firm. Stir in the liqueur or brandy.

three Spoon the mascarpone on to serving plates, top with the fruit and juices and serve warm.

broiled peaches with brown sugar brûlée

4 large juicy peaches
½ cup heavy cream
2 tsp. lemon juice
3 tbsp. unrefined powdered sugar
1 tbsp. sliced almonds

one Halve the peaches, remove the pits, and place, skin sides down, in a shallow flameproof dish.

two Mix the cream with the lemon juice and 1 tbsp. of the powdered sugar. Pour over the peaches. Sprinkle with the remaining powdered sugar, then the almonds.

three Cook under a preheated moderate broiler for about 5 minutes or until the sugar is bubbling and lightly caramelized. Serve warm.

Preparation time 5 minutes Cooking time 15 minutes Total time 20 minutes Makes 10

blueberry and vanilla patties

5 oz. ground almonds
½ cup plus 2 tbsp. golden brown sugar
½ cup self-rising flour
6 tbsp. unsalted butter, melted
4 egg whites
1 tsp. vanilla extract
1 cup blueberries

one Line 10 sections of a muffin tin with paper liners, or grease the tin. Mix together the ground almonds, sugar, flour, and butter. Add the egg whites and vanilla extract and mix to a smooth paste.

two Spoon into the liners and scatter with the blueberries.

three Bake in a preheated 425°F oven for 15 minutes until just firm in the center. Leave for 5 minutes, then transfer to a wire rack to cool.

Preparation time 10 minutes Cooking time 20 minutes Total time 30 minutes Serves 4

toffee apple muffin

3 dessert apples, cored and thickly sliced
¾ cup plus 2 tbsp. self-rising flour, plus
1 tablespoon extra
½ cup plus 2 tbsp. light brown sugar
¼ cup sugar
½ tsp. ground pumpkin pie spice
1 egg
7 tbsp. yogurt
2 tbsp. unsalted butter, melted

A great standby that few can resist! During cooking, the brown sugar melts to form a deliciously smooth, toffee-like sauce for the apples. It is perfect served with vanilla ice-cream.

one Toss the apples in a shallow ovenproof dish with the 1 tablespoonful of flour and the brown sugar.

two Mix the remaining flour with the sugar and spice in a bowl. Add the egg, yogurt, and butter and stir lightly until only just combined.

three Spoon the mixture over the apples and bake in a preheated 425°F oven for about 15–20 minutes until just firm and golden. Serve warm.

syrupy pears with chocolate crumble

¼ cup plus 1 tablespoon light brown sugar
¼ cup raisins
½ tsp. ground cinnamon
4 ripe dessert pears, peeled, halved, and cored
1½ tbsp. unsalted butter
½ cup rolled oats
¼ cup hazelnuts, coarsely chopped
2 oz. dark or milk chocolate, chopped
lightly whipped cream or yogurt, to serve (optional)

You need luscious, full-flavored dessert pears to make this pudding, which will soften quickly in the syrup.

one Place half of the sugar in a frying pan or wide sauté pan with ½ cup water and the raisins and cinnamon. Bring just to a boil, add the pears, and simmer gently, uncovered, for about 5 minutes or until the pears are slightly softened.

two Melt the butter in a separate frying pan or saucepan. Add the rolled oats and sauté gently for 2 minutes. Stir in the remaining sugar and cook over a gentle heat until golden.

three Spoon the pears on to serving plates. Stir the hazelnuts and chocolate into the oats mixture. Once the chocolate has melted, spoon over the pears. Serve topped with whipped cream or yogurt if desired.

chocolate cherry slices

14 oz. can black cherries in syrup
3 tbsp. Kirsch
1 tablespoon lemon juice
3½ oz. ricotta cheese
2 tbsp. powdered sugar
1 oz. plain chocolate, chopped
1 piece of bottled stem ginger, finely chopped
4 thick slices of moist chocolate cake

Bought chocolate cake can be dramatically transformed when bathed in liqueured syrup and topped with cherries, ricotta, and chocolate chunks.

one Thoroughly drain the cherries, reserving the syrup. Blend 4 tbsp. of the syrup with the Kirsch and lemon juice.

two Mix together the ricotta and powdered sugar in a bowl. Gently fold in the cherries, chocolate, and ginger.

three Place the chocolate cake on serving plates and spoon over the Kirsch syrup. Pile the cherry mixture on top.

index

A

apples: toffee apple muffin, 122
apricots: green couscous with spiced
    fruit sauce, 85
    pan-fried apricots with gingered
    mascarpone, 121
artichokes: kedgeree with rosemary
    butter and, 53
    tomato, artichoke, and mozzarella
    pizza, 62
asparagus, celeriac and potato
    remoulade with, 102
avocados: spiced orange and avocado
    salad, 97

B

basil and tomato stew, 108
beans, 35–45
    bean and beer casserole with baby
    dumplings, 45
    garlic, herb, and bean pâté, 36
    see also individual types of bean
beets: beet risotto with
    horseradish and mixed leaves, 56
    beet salad with cilantro and
    tomato salsa, 95
    couscous fritters with sour cream
    and, 83
black bean and cabbage stew, 38
black bean soup with soba noodles, 15
blueberry and vanilla patties, 122
broad beans, lemon, and
    parmesan risotto, 48
brown beans with lemon,
    parsley, and egg dressing, 45
bruschetta, goat cheese, onion, and
    pine nut, 61
bulgar wheat: tabbouleh with fruit and
    nuts, 87

C

cabbage: black bean and
    cabbage stew, 38
    spaghetti squash with cabbage
    and nuts, 105
cake, crispy, fried pasta, 32
Camembert and shallot tarts, 74
cannellini beans on toast, 43
carrots: carrot and potato rösti, 71
    ribboned carrot salad, 93
cauliflower crumble, buttered, 112
celeriac and potato remoulade with
    asparagus, 102
Cheddar burgers with cucumber
    salsa, 64
cheese, 8
    Camembert and shallot tarts, 74
Cheddar burgers with cucumber
    salsa, 64
cherry tomato and ricotta penne,
    24
chili cheese and corn cakes, 44
feta and tapenade drop scones, 75
phyllo, pesto, and mozzarella pockets,
    70
minted pea cake with mozzarella,
    tomato, and basil, 74
pasta with watercress, dolcelatte, and
    walnut sauce, 26
phyllo, pesto, and mozzarella
    pockets, 70
sage and walnut risotto with a
    cheese crust, 52
soft polenta with Gruyère and
    tomato sauce, 84
sweet potato, arugula, and haloumi
    salad, 93
see also goat cheese
zucchini and Parmesan soup, 21
zucchini pancakes with Swiss cheese
    and peppers, 71
cherries: chocolate cherry slices, 125
cherry tomato and ricotta penne, 24
cherry tomato tarts with pesto crème
    fraîche, 73
chestnuts: chestnut risotto cakes, 48
chickpeas: chickpea purée with eggs
    and spiced oil, 40
    falafel cakes, 73
chilies, 8
    chili and pimento soup, 20
    chili cheese and corn cakes, 44
chocolate: chocolate cherry slices, 125
    syrupy pears with chocolate
    crumble, 125
coconut, 8
coconut, creamed, 8
    coconut rice with peanut sauce, 55
    coconut rice with spiced
    vegetable, 55
coconut milk, 8
    pumpkin and coconut soup, 20
    red beans with coconut and
    cashews, 43
    vegetable noodles in spiced
    coconut milk, 31
couscous: couscous fritters with
    beet and sour cream, 83
    green couscous with spiced fruit
    sauce, 85
    mushroom, couscous, and herb
    sausages, 87
    spiced vegetable couscous, 84
cranberry, oatmeal, and cinnamon
    scones, 116
cranberry beans: nut koftas with
    minted yogurt, 36

crumble, buttered cauliflower, 112
cucumber salsa, 64

D

deviled mushrooms on brioche, 102

E

eggplant: eggplant pâté, 111
    grilled baby eggplant and tomato
    salad, 94
    fettucine with pine nuts and, 24
    tortillas with minted chili yogurt
    and eggplant, 66
eggs: chickpea purée with eggs and
    spiced oil, 40
    garlic and paprika soup with a
    floating egg, 18
    kedgeree with artichokes and
    rosemary butter, 53
    spinach and egg muffins with
    mustard hollandaise, 61
    watercress and mushroom frittata, 108

F

falafel cakes, 73
feta and tapenade drop scones, 75
fettuccine with eggplant and
    pine nuts, 24
fettuccine with tomatoes and
    tapenade, 26
flageolet beans: garlic, herb, and bean
    pâté, 36
    green couscous with spiced fruit
    sauce, 85
French beans: potato and French bean
    salad, 98
frittata, watercress and mushroom, 108
fritters, couscous, with beet and
    sour cream, 83

G

garlic and paprika soup with a floating
    egg, 18
garlic, herb, and bean pâté, 36
ginger and parsnip soup, fresh, 17
goat cheese: goat cheese linguini
    with garlic and herb butter, 28
    goat cheese, onion and pine nut
    bruschetta, 61
    toasted goat cheese with sun-dried
    tomato pesto, 65
grapes, herb salad with stem ginger
    and, 97
green beans, rice noodles with ginger
    and, 31
    salad with potato and, 98

green couscous with spiced fruit sauce, 85
green lentil soup with spiced butter, 12

H

herb salad with stem ginger and grapes, 97

J

Japanese rice with nori, 50

K

kedgeree with artichokes and rosemary butter, 53
koftas, nut, with minted yogurt, 36

L

lasagne, mushroom, zucchini and mascarpone, 27
leeks: new potato, cilantro and leek soup, 15
lemon grass, 8
    lemon grass and tofu nuggets with chili sauce, 77
lemon rice with feta and chargrilled peppers, 56
lentils: braised lentils with mushrooms and gremolata, 38
    green lentil soup with spiced butter, 12
    red lentil dhal with okra, 39
lima beans: lima bean and sun-dried tomato soup, 12
linguini: goats cheese linguini with garlic and herb butter, 28

M

minted pea cake with mozzarella, tomato, and basil, 74
muffins: spinach and egg muffins with mustard hollandaise, 61
    toffee apple muffin, 122
mushrooms: eggplant pâté, 111
    braised lentils with mushrooms and gremolata, 38
    deviled mushrooms on brioche, 102
    mushroom, zucchini and mascarpone lasagne, 27
    mushroom, couscous, and herb sausages, 87
    mushroom toad-in-the-hole with beer and onion gravy, 105
    polenta fries with saffron mushrooms, 88
    spinach and mushroom soup, 16

watercress and mushroom frittata, 108

N

noodles, 8
    black bean soup with soba noodles, 15
    rice noodle pancakes with stir-fried vegetables, 32
    rice noodles with green beans and ginger, 31
    stir-fried vegetable noodles, 28
    vegetable noodles in spiced coconut milk, 31
nori, Japanese rice with, 50

O

oats: chunky oat cookies, 119
    cranberry, oatmeal, and cinnamon scones, 116
okra, red lentil dhal with, 39
olive oil, 8
oranges: spiced orange and avocado salad, 97

P

pancakes: zucchini pancakes with Swiss cheese and peppers, 71
    rice noodle pancakes with stir-fried vegetables, 32
    vegetable rice pancakes with sesame and ginger sauce, 78
panzanella, 98
parsnips: fresh ginger and parsnip soup, 17
pasta, 8–9
    cherry tomato and ricotta penne, 24
    crispy fried pasta cake, 32
    fettuccine with eggplant and pine nuts, 24
    fettuccine with tomatoes and tapenade, 26
    goat cheese linguini with garlic and herb butter, 28
    mushroom, zucchini, and mascarpone lasagne, 27
    pasta with watercress, dolcelatte, and walnut sauce, 26
pastries: phyllo, pesto, and mozzarella pockets, 70
    tofu, cinnamon, and honey pockets, 75
pâtés: eggplant pâté, 111
    garlic, herb, and bean pâté, 36
peaches: grilled peaches with brown sugar brûlée, 121

pears: syrupy pears with chocolate crumble, 125
peas: minted pea cake with mozzarella, tomato, and basil, 74
penne, cherry tomato and ricotta, 24
peppers:
    lemon rice with feta and chargrilled peppers, 56
    panzanella, 98
    red bean and pepper cakes with lemon mayonnaise, 44
    red rice and pepper pilaf, 49
    zucchini pancakes with swiss cheese and peppers, 71
pesto, 9
phyllo, pesto and mozzarella pockets, 70
pilaf: red rice and pepper pilaf, 49
    spiced pilaf with pickled walnuts, 50
pizzas: spinach, onion and cream cheese pizza, 60
    tomato, artichoke and mozzarella pizza, 62
plum and amaretto tartlets, 118
polenta, 9
    polenta fries with saffron mushrooms, 88
    soft polenta with Gruyère and tomato sauce, 84
potatoes: carrot and potato rösti, 71
    celeriac and potato remoulade with asparagus, 102
    creamed corn and potato soup, 16
    minted pea cake with mozzarella, tomato, and basil, 74
    new potato, cilantro and leek soup, 15
    potato and green bean salad, 98
prunes: tabbouleh with fruit and nuts, 87
pumpkin and coconut soup, 20

R

red kidney beans: baby squash with red bean sauce, 107
    red bean and pepper cakes with lemon mayonnaise, 44
    red beans with coconut and cashews, 43
refried beans, tortilla wraps with cilantro relish and, 64
ribboned carrot salad, 93
rice, 9, 47–57
    beet risotto with horseradish and mixed leaves, 56
    chestnut risotto cakes, 48
    coconut rice with peanut sauce, 55
    coconut rice, with spiced vegetable, 55

index

fava bean, lemon, and Parmesan
    risotto, 48
Japanese rice with nori, 50
kedgeree with artichokes and
    rosemary butter, 53
lemon rice with feta and
    chargrilled peppers, 56
red rice and pepper pilaf, 49
sage and walnut risotto with a
    cheese crust, 52
spiced pilaf with pickled walnuts, 50
spiced vegetable biryani, 55
rice noodle pancakes with stir-fried
    vegetables, 32
rice noodles with green beans and
    ginger, 31
root vegetables: pan-fried roots with
    cardamom and honey, 113
rösti, carrot and potato, 71

S

saffron, 9
sage and walnut risotto with a cheese
    crust, 52
salads, 91–9
    beet salad with cilantro and
        tomato salsa, 95
    brown beans with lemon, parsley and
        egg dressing, 45
    grilled baby eggplant and tomato
        salad, 94
    herb salad with stem ginger and
        grapes, 97
    panzanella, 98
    potato and green bean salad, 98
    ribboned carrot salad, 93
    spiced orange and avocado salad, 97
    sweet potato, arugula, and haloumi
        salad, 93
    Thai-dressed tofu rolls, 95
sausages, mushroom, couscous and
    herb, 87
scones: cranberry, oatmeal, and
    cinnamon scones, 116
    feta and tapenade drop scones, 75
shallots: creamed shallot and rosemary
    soup, 18
soba noodles, black bean soup with,
    15
soups, 11–21
    black bean soup with soba
        noodles, 15
    chili and pimento soup, 20
    creamed corn and potato soup, 16
    creamed shallot and rosemary
        soup, 18
    fresh ginger and parsnip soup, 17
    garlic and paprika soup with a
        floating egg, 18

green lentil soup with spiced
    butter, 12
lima bean and sun-dried tomato
    soup, 12
new potato, cilantro, and
    leek soup, 15
pumpkin and coconut soup, 20
spinach and mushroom soup, 16
zucchini and Parmesan soup, 21
spaghetti squash with cabbage and
    nuts, 105
spinach: spinach and egg muffins with
    mustard hollandaise, 61
    spinach and mushroom soup, 16
    spinach, onion, and cream cheese
        pizza, 60
    wilted spinach with pine nuts and
        raisins, 104
squash: baby squash with red bean
    sauce, 107
    spaghetti squash with cabbage and
        nuts, 105
stew, basil and tomato, 108
stock, vegetable, 9
sun-dried tomatoes, 9
sweet potato, arugula, and
    haloumi salad, 93
sweetcorn: chili cheese and
    corn cakes, 44
    creamed corn and potato soup, 16
syrupy pears with chocolate
    crumble, 125

T

tabbouleh with fruit and nuts, 87
tapenade, 9
    fettuccine with tomatoes and, 26
tarts: Camembert and shallot tarts,
    74
    cherry tomato tarts with pesto crème
        fraîche, 73
    plum and amaretto tartlets, 118
Thai-dressed tofu rolls, 95
tiramisu, quick, 119
toad-in-the-hole, mushroom, with beer
    and onion gravy, 105
tofu, 9
    lemon grass and tofu with
        chili sauce, 77
    Thai-dressed tofu rolls, 95
    tofu, cinnamon, and honey pockets,
        75
tomatoes: baked vine tomatoes with
    garlic and herbs, 109
    basil and tomato stew, 108
    beet salad with cilantro and
        tomato salsa, 95
    cannellini beans on toast, 43
    cherry tomato and ricotta penne, 24

cherry tomato tarts with pesto crème
    fraîche, 73
grilled baby eggplant and tomato
    salad, 94
lima bean and sun-dried tomato
    soup, 12
fettuccine with tomatoes and
    tapenade, 26
sun-dried tomatoes, 9
toasted goat cheese with sun-dried
    tomato pesto, 65
tomato, artichoke, and mozzarella
    pizza, 62
tortillas: tortilla wraps with refried
    beans and cilantro relish, 64
    tortillas with minted chili yogurt
        and eggplant, 66

V

vegetables: pan-fried roots with
    cardamom and honey, 113
    rice noodle pancakes with stir-fried
        vegetables, 32
    spiced vegetable biryani, 55
    spiced vegetable couscous, 84
    stir-fried vegetable noodles, 28
    stock, 9
    vegetable chips, 112
    vegetable noodles in spiced coconut
        milk, 31
    vegetable rice pancakes with sesame
        and ginger sauce, 78
vinegar, balsamic, 8

W

walnuts: spiced pilaf with pickled
    walnuts, 50
watercress: pasta with watercress,
    dolcelatte, and walnut sauce, 26
    watercress and mushroom
        frittata, 108

Y

yogurt, deep-fried zucchini with
    minted, 104
    nut koftas with minted, 36

Z

zucchini:
    zucchini and Parmesan soup, 21
    zucchini pancakes with Emmental
        and peppers, 71
    deep-fried zucchini with minted
        yogurt, 104
    mushroom, zucchini and
        mascarpone lasagne, 27